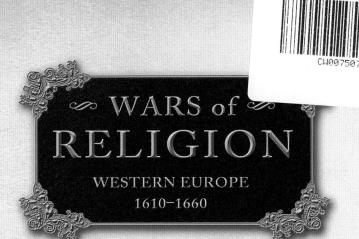

WARS of RELIGION
WESTERN EUROPE
1610–1660

Written by Nik Gaukroger and
Richard Bodley Scott, assisted by
Paul Robinson, Karsten Loh, David Caceres,
Xavier Codina, John Munro and Mike Kroon

OSPREY
PUBLISHING

SLITHERINE

First published in Great Britain in 2010 by Osprey Publishing Ltd.

© 2010 Osprey Publishing Ltd and Slitherine Software UK Ltd.

Osprey Publishing
Midland House, West Way, Botley, Oxford OX2 0PH, UK
44–02 23rd St, Suite 219, Long Island City, NY 11101, USA
E-mail: info@ospreypublishing.com

Slitherine Software UK Ltd
The White Cottage, 8 West Hill Avenue, Epsom, KT19 8LE, UK
E-mail: info@slitherine.co.uk

A CIP catalogue record for this book is available from the
British Library

ISBN: 978 1 84908 225 9
E-book ISBN: 978 1 84908 226 6

Cover concept and page layout by Myriam Bell Design, France
Typeset in Adobe Caslon Pro
Cover artwork by Peter Dennis
Photography supplied by Warlord Games, Ancient & Modern
Army Supplies/Donnington Miniatures, Testudo, Juergen Mueller,
Igwarg, Richard Ellis, Mark Sieber, Old Glory UK, Wargames
Illustrated
Project management by JD McNeil and Osprey Team
Technical management by Iain McNeil
Originated by PDQ Media, UK
Printed in China through Worldprint Ltd

10 11 12 13 14   10 9 8 7 6 5 4 3 2 1

Osprey Publishing is supporting the Woodland Trust, the UK's
leading woodland conservation charity, by funding the dedication
of trees.

CONTENTS

INTRODUCTION

The history of Western Europe in the first half of the 17th century is dominated by the great conflict known as the Thirty Years' War, although in reality it may be better to view it as a series of related conflicts rather than a single whole. Starting in 1618, and fought mainly in modern day Germany, its influence was felt as far west as Ireland, and filtered eastwards through Poland and Hungary.

The causes of the war go back to the start of the Reformation in the early 16th century, when the authority of the Catholic Church was questioned and rejected by thinkers such as Martin Luther and John Calvin. The Reformed Religion, or Religions, were adopted by many of the Princes of the Holy Roman Empire, which did nothing to help what was already a rather disunited political entity. However, around the middle of the century a formula was reached whereby the various states within the Empire could coexist regardless of their nominal religion, and so Germany stayed more or less at peace for over half a century.

By the start of the 17th century things had started to change. Not only had the Catholic "counter-reformation" got underway, but the Habsburg Emperors of the time, heavily influenced by their Jesuit confessors, saw it as their ordained duty to re-impose Catholicism on their subjects. Unsurprisingly, the Protestant Princes were somewhat worried by this turn of events and tensions within the Empire rose.

The event that was to push things over the edge and ignite the war that was to rage for thirty years, was the election of Frederick V, the Elector Palatine, to the throne of Bohemia by the Bohemian estates, who were in revolt against the Habsburgs. The resulting war is traditionally split into four phases: the Bohemian revolt, the Danish intervention, the Swedish phase and the French phase, each named after the state which acted so as to continue the war at that point. From its starting point in Bohemia it expanded to cover all of Germany, taking in the latter stages of the Spanish-Dutch Eighty Years' War and the ongoing rivalry and conflict that was endemic between the French and both Habsburg family branches ruling in Austria and Spain.

Although largely fought in Germany, by German soldiers in the pay of various masters, the war drew in large numbers of men from the Low Countries, France, Denmark, Sweden, Spain and the British Isles as the conflict escalated into a pan-European war. Additionally, soldiers from Hungary and Transylvania in Eastern Europe played an important role in the early stages of the war, and remained a factor until the final resolution in 1648.

Inevitably, such a prolonged war, fought over the same area for so long, caused a huge amount of suffering and loss. Parts of Germany, especially, suffered periods of extreme devastation as armies crossed, and recrossed, the countryside. With the universal use of the system of "contributions", in reality forced exactions, to supply armies both on the march and when they were in quarters, there was a strong economic incentive to fight the war outside of your own borders, so that the enemy paid for both your army and his own. However, it must be remembered that even areas outside of the immediate war zone could suffer. For example Sweden, with its low population, sent a very high proportion of its male workforce to the war, which impacted heavily on the population that remained at home.

The Earl of Essex takes command!

In terms of military technology the Thirty Years' War produced little that was new. All the weapons used in the war existed before it started, and would remain in use after it ended. However, the period did see the musket coming to the fore as the most important infantry weapon, as the decisive effects of firepower started to be understood. This resulted in infantry formations becoming shallower than they had been in the 16th century, and the start of the development of linear tactics that would dominate the battlefield for the next two centuries. A side effect of the increasing importance of firearms was the continued decline in the use of armour for personal protection.

This volume covers the armies that took part in the great European conflict of the Thirty Years' War and its associated peripheral wars such as the English Civil Wars and the Portuguese War of Restoration.

As you look at each army, you will find the following sections:

* Brief **historical notes** on the army, its wars, its famous generals, weapons and/or troop types.
* A ready-to-play **starter army** – just put it together and play a balanced small game.
* Instructions for building a **customised army** using our points system.
* A table with the full list of **compulsory** and **optional** troops.

Although each of the army lists in this book contains useful historical notes, the Thirty Years' War is a very complex subject and it is impossible to fully do it justice in such a short space. Players who are interested in the wider history of the war, and its origins, are advised to buy one of the substantial studies of the war, such as the recently published "Europe's Tragedy", by Peter H. Wilson.

Pikemen

LATER EIGHTY YEARS' WAR DUTCH

The rebellion of the Dutch provinces against their Spanish overlords broke out in 1568, It was initially, on the whole, a military disaster, with the Dutch unable to stand in the field against the veteran Spanish tercios. As a result, the war descended into a series of sieges of the many fortified towns and cities in the Low Countries.

Around 1590, partly inspired by classical works by authors such as Aelian and Vegetius, Maurice and William Louis of Nassau began to reform the army. The cavalry were converted from lancers and mercenary reiters into charging cuirassiers who used their pistols as close combat weapons rather than missile weapons. In this they may have been partly inspired by the reforms of the Huguenot cavalry by Henri of Navarre (Henri IV of France), some of whom served as volunteers in the Dutch army. Additionally, the infantry were reorganised into smaller, handier, battlefield formations called "hopen", which were formed by dividing larger regiments, or by combining companies of smaller regiments.

Despite these undoubted improvements, field battles remained rare, with encounters such as Nieuwpoort in 1600 being very much the exception rather than the rule. However, by maintaining a credible army in being, the Dutch forced the Spanish to likewise maintain a large force in the field. This, given the parlous state of Spanish finances, worked to the advantage of the Dutch, as they were better placed economically to endure a prolonged war. Indeed, the Spanish crown was forced to admit to bankruptcy on more than one occasion, and was chronically unable to pay its troops regularly, unlike the Dutch, and so suffered constant desertions as a result - often to the Dutch, who promptly enrolled such troops in their army.

By 1609 both sides were exhausted and needed peace, but the Spanish could not yet face up to losing the valuable provinces, and so a 12-year truce was agreed and the two sides dramatically reduced their armies. By the time the truce expired in 1621, the Dutch had become involved in the opening stages of the Thirty Years' War by their support of their fellow Protestants in the Rhine Palatinate. An attempt was made to extend the truce, but this was a failure and war with Spain was resumed.

As previously, the war in the Low Countries was marked by a lack of field battles, and was again a series of sieges and manoeuvres by the respective armies with, from 1635, the Spanish being hampered by also fighting against the French. By the late 1640s the Spanish had finally come to accept that they would never regain control of the Dutch provinces, and peace was agreed between the Dutch Republic and Spain as part of the negotiations that brought the Thirty Years' War to an end.

This list covers the armies of the Dutch Republic from the military reforms of Maurice and William Louis of Nassau from 1590 until the Peace of Westphalia in 1648 ended both the Eighty and Thirty Years' Wars. The army of the initial revolt from 1568 until 1589 is covered in Field of Glory Renaissance Companion 2: *Trade and Treachery*.

Dutch veteran infantry

TROOP NOTES

Whilst Dutchmen were a minority in the armies of the United Provinces, the foreign troops, English, Scots and Germans in the main, were organised into Dutch style units and fought in the same manner as the Dutch. Some of the best regiments of the army were in fact foreign, such as the English foot (commanded by Sir Francis Vere) who performed so well at the Battle of Nieuwpoort in 1600.

In 1600 and 1603 large bodies of unpaid Spanish troops (in reality Walloons and Germans) deserted to the Dutch and were incorporated into the army in larger than usual regiments. We allow for the possibility that these may have briefly operated like tercios and thus allow them to use the Later Tercio rules. Despite being deserters, the unit in 1600 fought effectively at the Battle of Nieuwpoort and so justifies Average rating.

Cavalry formed a minor part of the army owing to the nature of the terrain in the Low Countries. Maurice and William Louis converted the lance armed cavalry into cuirassiers although a few lancers are recorded as late as 1600. The new cuirassiers formed the majority of the Dutch cavalry and were supported by less well armoured "Arquebusiers". It is unclear whether the Dutch followed the trends of the rest of Europe and lightened their cavalry equipment during the Thirty Years' War, but we allow for the possibility.

The shot component of the foot regiments were initially armed with a mixture of arquebus and muskets, with the latter replacing the former over time. We give battle groups the capability of the majority weapon type. However, some Walloon regiments may have been predominantly musket armed even in the early part of this list and, therefore, we allow a small number of musket armed battle groups at this time as well as the majority arquebus armed.

LATER EIGHTY YEARS' WAR DUTCH STARTER ARMY		
Commander-in-Chief	1	Field Commander
Sub-commanders	2	2 x Troop Commander
Cuirassiers	2 BGs	Each comprising 4 bases of cuirassiers: Superior, Heavily Armoured, Horse – Impact Pistol, Melee Pistol
Arquebusiers	1 BG	4 bases of arquebusiers: Average, Armoured, Horse – Carbine, Melee Pistol
Infantry Hopen	6 BGs	Each comprising 6 bases of infantry hopen: 2 Average, Armoured, Heavy Foot – Pike; and 4 Average, Unarmoured, Medium Foot – Musket
Field Guns	1 BG	2 bases of field artillery: Average, Medium Artillery – Medium Artillery
Camp	1	Unfortified camp
Total	10 BGs	Camp, 12 mounted bases, 38 foot bases, 3 commanders

BUILDING A CUSTOMISED LIST USING OUR ARMY POINTS

Choose an army based on the maxima and minima in the list below. The following special instructions apply to this army:

- Commanders should be depicted as cuirassiers.
- French allies cannot be used with Swedes and Hessians.
- Battle groups designated as "(LT)" count as later tercios as defined in the rule book.

LATER EIGHTY YEARS' WAR DUTCH

Territory Types: Agricultural

C-in-C		Great Commander/Field Commander/Troop Commander					80/50/35		1	
Sub-commanders		Field Commander					50		0–2	
		Troop Commander					35		0–3	
Troop name		Troop Type			Capabilities			Points per base	Bases per BG	Total bases
		Type	Armour	Quality	Shooting	Impact	Melee			
Core Troops										
Lancers	Only before 1601	Horse	Heavily Armoured	Superior	–	Heavy Lancers	Swordsmen	16	4	0–4
Cuirassiers	Any date	Horse	Heavily Armoured	Superior	–	Pistol	Pistol	16	4	0–12 / 4–12
	Only from 1640	Horse	Armoured	Superior	–	Pistol	Pistol	13	4	
Arquebusiers		Horse	Armoured	Average	Carbine	–	Pistol	11	4–6	4–8
			Unarmoured					9		
Infantry *Hopen*	Only before 1610	Medium Foot	Unarmoured	Average	Arquebus	–	–	7	4	6 / 12–102
		Heavy Foot	Armoured	Average	–	Pike	Pike	6	2	
	Only from 1610	Medium Foot	Unarmoured	Average	Musket	–	–	8	4	6
		Heavy Foot	Armoured	Average	–	Pike	Pike	6	2	
Field Guns		Medium Artillery	–	Average	Medium Artillery	–	–	20	2, 3 or 4	2–6 / 2–6
		Heavy Artillery	–	Average	Heavy Artillery	–	–	25	2	0–2
Optional Troops										
Veteran infantry regiments	Only before 1610	Medium Foot	Unarmoured	Superior	Arquebus	–	–	10	4	6 / 0–18
		Heavy Foot	Armoured	Superior	–	Pike	Pike	9	2	
Walloon regiments		Medium Foot	Unarmoured	Average	Musket	–	–	8	4	6 / 0–12
		Heavy Foot	Armoured	Average	–	Pike	Pike	6	2	
Dragoons		Dragoons	Unarmoured	Average	Musket	–	–	8	2	0–2
Warships		Naval Units	–	Average	Naval	–	–	30	–	0–2
Field defences		Field Fortifications	–	–	–	–	–	–	–	0–24
Allies										
English allies (only before 1595) – Elizabethan English (FOGR Companion 2: *Trade and Treachery*)										
French allies (only from 1621 to 1639) – Early 17th Century French (before 1635) or Thirty Years' War French (only from 1635)										
Special Campaigns										
Only in 1600 or 1603										
"Spanish" deserters		Medium Foot	Unarmoured	Average	Arquebus	–	–	7	6	9 (LT) / 0–9
		Heavy Foot	Armoured	Average	–	Pike	Pike	6	3	
Only in 1633										
Swedish allied commander		Field Commander/Troop Commander						40/25		1
Swedish *lätta ryttare*		Determined Horse	Armoured	Superior	–	Pistol	Pistol	21	4	4–12
Hessian cavalry		Horse	Armoured	Average	–	Pistol	Pistol	10	4	4
		Horse	Armoured	Average	Carbine	–	Pistol	11	4	
			Unarmoured					9		

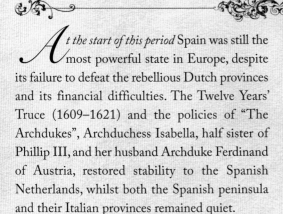

LATER EIGHTY YEARS' WAR DUTCH ALLIES										
Allied commander		Field Commander/Troop Commander					40/25		1	
Sub-commanders		Field Commander					50		0–2	
		Troop Commander					35		0–3	
Troop name		Troop Type			Capabilities			Points per base	Bases per BG	Total bases
		Type	Armour	Quality	Shooting	Impact	Melee			
Cuirassiers	Any date	Horse	Heavily Armoured	Superior	–	Pistol	Pistol	16	4	0–8 4–8
	Only from 1640	Horse	Armoured	Superior	–	Pistol	Pistol	13	4	
Arquebusiers		Horse	Armoured	Average	Carbine	–	Pistol	11	4	0–4
			Unarmoured					9		
Infantry Hopen	Only before 1610	Medium Foot	Unarmoured	Average	Arquebus	–	–	7	4	6 12–30
		Heavy Foot	Armoured	Average	–	Pike	Pike	6	2	
	Only from 1610	Medium Foot	Unarmoured	Average	Musket	–	–	8	4	6
		Heavy Foot	Armoured	Average	–	Pike	Pike	6	2	
Field Guns		Medium Artillery	–	Average	Medium Artillery	–	–	20	2	0–2

LATER IMPERIAL SPANISH

*A*t the start of this period Spain was still the most powerful state in Europe, despite its failure to defeat the rebellious Dutch provinces and its financial difficulties. The Twelve Years' Truce (1609–1621) and the policies of "The Archdukes", Archduchess Isabella, half sister of Phillip III, and her husband Archduke Ferdinand of Austria, restored stability to the Spanish Netherlands, whilst both the Spanish peninsula and their Italian provinces remained quiet.

With the resumption of the war, the Spanish made a major effort to extinguish the Dutch Republic, attacking it both on land and at sea in an attempt to strangle the Dutch economy, which relied heavily on sea trade. This spread to the colonies and trading posts of both sides around the world.

At the same time the Spanish intervened in the growing conflict of the Thirty Years' War, both to enhance their own position in the Netherlands,

and also to assist their Austrian Habsburg cousins in their struggles with a series of Protestant enemies. Additionally, there were a series of minor wars in Italy to resolve local issues in the favour of their Italian satellite states, which also brought them into conflict with a re-emerging France, a fight that would have serious repercussions for Spain in the longer term.

By 1634, in the aftermath of Breitenfeld, Lützen and the death of Wallenstein, with the Swedes running rampant across Germany and the Dutch still unconquered, the Spanish decided that they needed to send major reinforcements to the Low Countries, but also with an eye to their use to assist the Emperor. Collecting the best of the Spanish forces in Italy, the Cardinal-Infante, Don Fernando, led them along the "Spanish Road" into Germany where he joined with his cousin, Ferdinand of Hungary (later Emperor). Together they achieved a crushing victory at Nördlingen,

which in a single day reversed all the gains of the Swedes in the preceding years, putting the Catholic forces into the ascendant for a number of years. However, possibly the main effect of this victory was that it drew France into committing its armies into the mainstream of the Thirty Years' War. The net result was that for the next decade, the Spanish would be fighting the French at the same time as fighting the Dutch.

Despite now fighting a war on at least two, and often three, fronts in France, the Low Countries and Southern Germany, the Spanish were still the dominant military force in the area. Indeed in 1636 the Spanish overran northern France after the capture of Corbie, and were within striking distance of Paris – which might just have knocked France out of the war if the success had been followed up boldly. However, it was not, and thus the war with France continued for over 20 more years.

By the early 1640s the Spanish were very much focused on the wars with the Dutch and France and had more or less withdrawn from the war in Germany. The war with France swung to and fro, with victories and defeats on both sides, although in general the Spanish had the better of these. Often seen as a turning point in the war, the Battle of Rocroi in 1643 was not as decisive as French mythology has made out, although it did see the destruction of the most effective units of the Spanish infantry.

Although both the Eighty and Thirty Years' Wars were brought to a conclusion in 1648 by the Peace of Westphalia, the war between Spain and France continued until the Peace of the Pyrenees in 1659. By this time it was clear that Spain was utterly exhausted, again bankrupt, and now eclipsed as the major power in Europe.

This list covers Spanish armies in the Low Countries from the end of the Twelve Years' Truce in 1621 until the Peace of the Pyrenees in 1659 confirmed Spanish decline in Europe. It also includes Spanish armies in Italy, or from Italy, such as that the Cardinal-Infante Don Fernando led to the Low Countries via the victory at Nördlingen in 1634.

TROOP NOTES

The main strength of the Spanish army was still the famous infantry tercio, but these went through a number of changes during this period.

When the Twelve Years' Truce expired in 1621 and the war against the Dutch flared up again, the Tercio was still, in theory, circa 3,000 men strong, but in practice actual numbers were roughly half of this. In 1632 an ordinance was issued that restated that the strength of a Tercio should be 3,000 men, however it directed that they should form up 10 ranks deep – this latter appears to be a case of bringing the theory in line with actual practice in the field rather than a radical reform, whilst the former remained an unattained ideal. Tercios of this size fought at Nördlingen. In our opinion these formations prior to 1635 should be treated as Later Tercios as defined in the rule book.

Subsequently the Tercio again declined in size, and by the time of the Battle of Rocroi in 1643 the actual size of individual units in the army of

Spanish Arquebusiers

Flanders was roughly 900 men. Montecuccoli, writing around this time, suggests that the normal fighting depth was now 7 ranks. These smaller formations are more akin to the "battalions", and similar, of other contemporary armies and thus in our opinion do not qualify to be treated as Later Tercios anymore, but as "other pike & shot formations" as defined in the rule book.

In addition to size and fighting formation, the weaponry of the Tercio went through changes as well. Up until at least the Battle of Nördlingen, the arquebus was still a common firearm in many units, and indeed remained so in the relative backwater of Italy subsequent to this. Before 1635, therefore, we allow a choice of firearm capability for many battle groups.

The Guardias viejas ("Old Guard"), the remnants of the old feudal nobility, may well have retained the lance until the Battle of Nördlingen in 1634, being subsequently re-equipped as cuirassiers, or they may have been cuirassiers for the whole period, Hence we allow both options. We assume that whenever they became cuirassiers they adopted the same fighting style as other Spanish cuirassiers, and they are included amongst the Caballos corazas in the Army of Flanders. As Spanish sources maintained that lancers were able to defeat pistol armed horse, the change may have been due to factors other than perceived effectiveness.

Caballos corazas could variously be equipped as heavily armoured cuirassiers or as lighter armoured demi-cuirassiers in the German fashion. The continued contact with the Swedes and Swedish influenced Germans from the mid-1630s may well have also led to shallower formations being adopted. Cavalry certainly became more important at this time in the Army of Flanders as its operations in France were in more cavalry friendly country; Italy, however, remained a military backwater.

The first dragoon company was created in 1632, and by the end of the period there were three units with a total establishment of 2600 men.

French rebel allies represent the troops of the Prince de Condé present at the second battle of the Dunes in 1658. Two battalions of English Royalist foot were also present fighting with the Spanish army.

LATER IMPERIAL SPANISH STARTER ARMY

Commander-in-Chief	1	Field Commander
Sub-commanders	2	2 x Troop Commander
Guardias viejas	1 BG	4 bases of guardias viejas: Superior, Heavily Armoured, Horse – Impact Pistol, Melee Pistol
Caballos corazas	2 BGs	Each comprising 4 bases of caballos corazas: Average, Armoured, Horse – Impact Pistol, Melee Pistol
Arquebusiers	1 BG	4 bases of arquebusiers: Average, Armoured, Horse – Carbine, Melee Pistol
Spanish tercios (LT)	1 BG	9 bases of Spanish tercios: 3 Superior, Armoured, Heavy Foot – Pike; and 6 Superior, Unarmoured, Medium Foot – Musket (Later Tercio)
Spanish tercios (LT)	2 BGs	Each comprising 9 bases of Spanish tercios: 3 Average, Armoured, Heavy Foot – Pike; and 6 Average, Unarmoured, Medium Foot – Musket (Later Tercio)
Dragoons	1 BG	3 bases of dragoons: Average, Unarmoured, Dragoons – Musket
Field artillery	1 BG	2 bases of field artillery: Average Medium Artillery – Medium Artillery
Camp	1	Unfortified camp
Total	9 BGs	Camp, 16 mounted bases, 32 foot bases, 3 commanders

BUILDING A CUSTOMISED LIST USING OUR ARMY POINTS

Choose an army based on the maxima and minima in the list below. The following special instructions apply to this army:

- Commanders should be depicted as Guardias viejas or caballos corazas.

- The army of the Cardinal-Infante in 1634 is treated as if the "Army of Flanders" for the options it is allowed.
- Only battle groups designated as "(LT)" count as later tercios as defined in the rule book.
- If any English Royalists are used then French rebel allies must be.

LATER IMPERIAL SPANISH									
Territory Types: Agricultural									
C-in-C		Great Commander/Field Commander/Troop Commander					80/50/35	1	
Sub-commanders		Field Commander					50	0–2	
		Troop Commander					35	0–3	
Troop name		Troop Type			Capabilities		Points per base	Bases per BG	Total bases
		Type	Armour	Quality	Shooting	Combat	Melee		
Core Troops									
Guardias viejas	Only before 1635	Gendarmes	Heavily Armoured	Superior	–	Light Lancers	Swordsmen	21	2–4	0–4	4–8
		Horse	Heavily Armoured	Superior	–	Pistol	Pistol	16	4		
Caballos corazas	Only before 1635 or Army of Italy	Horse	Heavily Armoured	Superior	–	Pistol	Pistol	16	4	0–8	4–8
		Horse	Heavily Armoured	Average	–	Pistol	Pistol	12	4		
		Horse	Armoured	Average	–	Pistol	Pistol	10	4		
	Army of Flanders only from 1635	Horse	Heavily Armoured	Superior	–	Pistol	Pistol	16	4	4–12	
		Determined Horse	Armoured	Superior	–	Pistol	Pistol	21	4		
		Horse	Heavily Armoured	Average	–	Pistol	Pistol	12	4	4–12	
		Horse	Armoured	Average	–	Pistol	Pistol	10	4		
		Determined Horse	Armoured	Average	–	Pistol	Pistol	12	4		
Arquebusiers	Only before 1635 or Army of Italy	Horse	Armoured	Average	Carbine	–	Pistol	11	4–6	4–8
			Unarmoured					9		
	Army of Flanders only from 1635	Horse	Unarmoured	Average	Carbine	–	Pistol	9	4	0–8
Tercios viejos españoles	Only Army of Flanders before 1635	Medium Foot	Unarmoured	Elite	Musket	–	–	13	6	9 (LT)	0–12
		Heavy Foot	Armoured	Elite	–	Pike	Pike	11	3		
	Only Army of Flanders from 1635	Medium Foot	Unarmoured	Elite	Musket	–	–	13	4	6	
		Heavy Foot	Armoured	Elite	–	Pike	Pike	11	2		

LATER IMPERIAL SPANISH

Troop name	Condition	Type	Armour	Quality	Shooting	Impact	Melee	Points	Bases	BG size	Min–Max	Total
Other Spanish tercios and "Tercios de las Naciones"	Only Army of Italy	Medium Foot	Unarmoured	Superior	Arquebus	–	–	10	6	9 (LT)	0–27	9–90
		Heavy Foot	Armoured	Superior	–	Pike	Pike	9	3	(LT)		
		Medium Foot	Unarmoured	Average	Arquebus	–	–	7	6	9 (LT)	9–90	
		Heavy Foot	Armoured	Average	–	Pike	Pike	6	3	(LT)		
	Only Army of Flanders before 1635	Medium Foot	Unarmoured	Superior	Musket	–	–	11	6	9 (LT)	9–54	
		Heavy Foot	Armoured	Superior	–	Pike	Pike	9	3	(LT)		
		Medium Foot	Unarmoured	Average	Musket	–	–	8	6	9 (LT)		
		Heavy Foot	Armoured	Average	–	Pike	Pike	6	3	(LT)		
		Medium Foot	Unarmoured	Superior	Arquebus	–	–	10	6	9 (LT)		
		Heavy Foot	Armoured	Superior	–	Pike	Pike	9	3	(LT)		
		Medium Foot	Unarmoured	Average	Arquebus	–	–	7	6	9 (LT)		
		Heavy Foot	Armoured	Average	–	Pike	Pike	6	3	(LT)		
	Only Army of Flanders From 1635	Medium Foot	Unarmoured	Superior	Musket	–	–	11	4	6	6–54	
		Heavy Foot	Armoured	Superior	–	Pike	Pike	9	2	6		
		Medium Foot	Unarmoured	Average	Musket	–	–	8	4	6		
		Heavy Foot	Armoured	Average	–	Pike	Pike	6	2	6		
Other foreign regiments	Only before 1635	Medium Foot	Unarmoured	Average	Arquebus	–	–	7	4	6	0–24	
		Heavy Foot	Armoured	Average	–	Pike	Pike	6	2	6		
	Only before 1626	Medium Foot	Unarmoured	Average	Musket*	–	–	7	4	6		
		Heavy Foot	Armoured	Average	–	Pike	Pike	6	2	6		
	Only from 1626 to 1634	Medium Foot	Unarmoured	Average	Musket	–	–	8	4	6		
		Heavy Foot	Armoured	Average	–	Pike	Pike	6	2	6		
	Only from 1635	Medium Foot	Unarmoured	Average	Musket	–	–	8	4	6	6–36	
		Heavy Foot	Unarmoured	Average	–	Pike	Pike	5	2	6		
Field guns		Medium Artillery	–	Average	Medium Artillery	–	–	20	2, 3 or 4		2–6	
Heavy guns		Heavy Artillery	–	Average	Heavy Artillery	–	–	25	2			

Optional Troops											
Dragoons	Only from 1632	Dragoons	Unarmoured	Average	Musket	–	–	8	3 or 4	0–6
Austrian Habsburg supplied Croats or similar		Light Horse	Unarmoured	Average	Carbine	–	Pistol	9	4–6	0–8
		Light Horse	Unarmoured	Average	Carbine	–	–	7	4–6	
Breastworks and redoubts		Field Fortifications	–	–	–	–	–	3	–	0–24

Allies

Imperialist allies (only from 1632 to 1639) – Later Thirty Years' War German (Imperial options)

Special Campaigns

Only joint Imperial–Spanish army at Nördlingen in 1634

Up to 1/2 of the army's points can be spent on troops from the Later Thirty Years' War German army list (Imperial options). Minima must be adhered to, but otherwise any eligible troops may be selected. No allies are allowed. All generals count in line of command to all troops in the army.

Only in Flanders in 1658

French rebel allies (only in 1658) – Early Louis XIV French

English Royalist Foot		Medium Foot	Unarmoured	Average	Musket	–	–	8	4	6	0–12
		Heavy Foot	Unarmoured	Average	–	Pike	Pike	5	2		

LATER IMPERIAL SPANISH ALLIES

Troop name		Troop Type			Capabilities			Points per base	Bases per BG		Total bases
Allied commander		Field Commander/Troop Commander						40/25	1		
		Type	Armour	Quality	Shooting	Combat	Melee				
Caballos corazas	Only before 1635 or Army of Italy	Horse	Heavily Armoured	Superior	–	Pistol	Pistol	16	4		0–4
		Horse	Heavily Armoured	Average	–	Pistol	Pistol	12	4		4
		Horse	Armoured	Average	–	Pistol	Pistol	10	4		
	Army of Flanders only from 1635	Horse	Heavily Armoured	Superior	–	Pistol	Pistol	16	4		4–8
		Determined Horse	Armoured	Superior	–	Pistol	Pistol	21	4		
		Horse	Heavily Armoured	Average	–	Pistol	Pistol	12	4		4–8
		Horse	Armoured	Average	–	Pistol	Pistol	10	4		
		Determined Horse	Armoured	Average	–	Pistol	Pistol	12	4		
Arquebusiers		Horse	Armoured	Average	Carbine	–	Pistol	11	4		0–4
			Unarmoured					9			
Other Spanish tercios and *"Tercios de las Naciones"*	Only Army of Italy	Medium Foot	Unarmoured	Superior	Arquebus	–	–	10	6	9	0–9
		Heavy Foot	Armoured	Superior	–	Pike	Pike	9	3	(LT)	9–36
		Medium Foot	Unarmoured	Average	Arquebus	–	–	7	6	9	9–36
		Heavy Foot	Armoured	Average	–	Pike	Pike	6	3	(LT)	
	Only Army of Flanders before 1635	Medium Foot	Unarmoured	Superior	Musket	–	–	11	6	9	9–30
		Heavy Foot	Armoured	Superior	–	Pike	Pike	9	3	(LT)	
		Medium Foot	Unarmoured	Average	Musket	–	–	8	6	9	
		Heavy Foot	Armoured	Average	–	Pike	Pike	6	3	(LT)	
		Medium Foot	Unarmoured	Superior	Arquebus	–	–	10	6	9	
		Heavy Foot	Armoured	Superior	–	Pike	Pike	9	3	(LT)	
		Medium Foot	Unarmoured	Average	Arquebus	–	–	7	6	9	
		Heavy Foot	Armoured	Average	–	Pike	Pike	6	3	(LT)	
Other Spanish tercios and *"Tercios de las Naciones"*	Only Army of Flanders From 1635	Medium Foot	Unarmoured	Superior	Musket	–	–	11	4	6	
		Heavy Foot	Armoured	Superior	–	Pike	Pike	9	2		
		Medium Foot	Unarmoured	Average	Musket	–	–	8	4	6	
		Heavy Foot	Armoured	Average	–	Pike	Pike	6	2		
Other foreign regiments	Only before 1635	Medium Foot	Unarmoured	Average	Arquebus	–	–	7	4	6	0–12
		Heavy Foot	Armoured	Average	–	Pike	Pike	6	2		
	Only before 1626	Medium Foot	Unarmoured	Average	Musket*	–	–	7	4	6	
		Heavy Foot	Armoured	Average	–	Pike	Pike	6	2		
	Only from 1626 to 1634	Medium Foot	Unarmoured	Average	Musket	–	–	8	4	6	
		Heavy Foot	Armoured	Average	–	Pike	Pike	6	2		
	Only from 1635	Medium Foot	Unarmoured	Average	Musket	–	–	8	4	6	
		Heavy Foot	Unarmoured	Average	–	Pike	Pike	5	2		
Field guns		Medium Artillery	–	Average	Medium Artillery	–	–	20	2		0–2

EARLY 17TH CENTURY FRENCH

*W*ith the assassination of Henri IV on the eve of a declaration of war against Spain, France remained somewhat inward looking and militarily weak with the ascension of the eight-year-old Louis XIII to the throne with his mother, Marie de Medici, as regent. Although he legally came of age when he reached the age of thirteen, it wasn't until some years later that he finally threw off the influence of his mother,

The first conflicts of Louis' reign were to be internal. A rebellion by a number of nobles in 1620 was easily suppressed by royal forces, but this was followed by troubles with the Protestant Huguenots within France, supported, albeit ineffectively, by England.

Following the rise of Armand Jean du Plessis de Richelieu, Cardinal-Duc de Richelieu, to the position of the King's first minister in 1624, France entered a period of stability and started once again to look to its interests on the international stage, especially in regard to its traditional rivals, the Habsburgs. With borders with Spain in both the Pyrenees and the Low Countries, plus the growing ascendancy of the Austrian Habsburgs in the Thirty Years' War, the French feared

Enfants perdus led by King's Musketeers

encirclement. To counter this they intervened with armies in Piedmont and northern Italy, in an attempt to break the so called "Spanish Road" that linked Spain's Italian possessions with the Low Countries, and also, more covertly, by financial support for the Dutch and German Protestants.

It was in this period that the Musketeers of the Guard, as made famous by Alexandre Dumas'"The Three Musketeers", were founded. Players may be interested to know that one Charles Ogier de Batz de Castelmore, Comte d'Artagnan, joined the company in 1632, possibly aided by the influence of a family friend, Jean-Armand du Peyrer, Comte de Troisville (or Tresville). D'Artagnan rose to the rank of captain of the company and was killed at the siege of Maastricht in 1673.

This list covers French armies from the assassination of Henri IV in 1610 until the entry of French armies into the main Thirty Years' War conflict in 1635.

TROOP NOTES

The pikemen of the Guard infantry regiments and the established Vieux and Petits Vieux regiments appear to have remained armoured in this period, but more ephemeral regiments and militia were probably not so well equipped.

French shot retained the arquebus in significant numbers for a much longer period than did their contemporaries, possibly due to relative peace at the start of the century. After 1622, however, the musket was the only firearm used by the infantry.

During this period French infantry increasingly favoured a rapid advance to close combat, rather than a fire fight maybe followed by close combat, as was more usual at the time. This behaviour developed during the early 1620s during the internal wars of the reign of Louis XIII. It even extended to attacking enemy in well prepared defences. Indeed one opposing general stated about a position attacked by the French: "*We were entrenched in places that I believed approachable only by the birds; we had covered the entire mountain with tree trunks that we had pushed down the slope; we were fortified in different places and covered by a number of forts.*" To represent this tendency from 1623 we limit French infantry to Musket* capability but give them Impact Foot capability in addition.

The Musketeers of the Guard were formed as mounted Carabins in 1622 and were part of the Maison du Roi. They fought both mounted and on foot, and were occasionally attached to the Enfants Perdu for especially hazardous missions, in which role they were considered superior to all other troops. Thus we rate such Musketeer led bodies as Superior, and the battle group bases of such should include dismounted Musketeers figures in addition to normal musketeers.

EARLY 17TH CENTURY FRENCH STARTER ARMY		
Commander-in-Chief	1	Field Commander
Sub-commanders	2	2 x Troop Commander
Cuirassiers	2 BGs	Each comprising 4 bases of cuirassiers: Superior, Heavily Armoured, Horse – Impact Pistol, Melee Pistol
Chevaux-légers	1 BG	4 bases of chevaux-légers: Average, Armoured, Horse – Impact Pistol, Melee Pistol
Forlorn Hope Carabins	1 BG	4 bases of forlorn hope carabins: Average, Unarmoured, Light Horse – Carbine, Melee Pistol
Veteran guard infantry	1 BG	6 bases of veteran guard infantry: 2 Superior, Armoured, Heavy Foot – Pike; and 4 Superior, Unarmoured, Medium Foot – Musket*, Impact Foot
Vieux Infantry	3 BGs	Each comprising 6 bases of vieux infantry: 2 Average, Armoured, Heavy Foot – Pike; and 4 Average, Unarmoured, Medium Foot – Musket*, Impact Foot
Foreign Infantry Regiments	1 BG	6 bases of foreign infantry regiments: 2 Average, Armoured, Heavy Foot – Pike; and 4 Average, Unarmoured, Medium Foot – Musket
Field artillery	1 BG	3 bases of field artillery: Average, Light Artillery – Light Artillery
Camp	1	Unfortified camp
Total	10 BGs	Camp, 16 mounted bases, 33 foot bases, 3 commanders

BUILDING A CUSTOMISED LIST USING OUR ARMY POINTS

Choose an army based on the maxima and minima in the list below. The following special instructions apply to this army:

- Commanders should be depicted as Cuirassiers.
- Only one allied contingent may be fielded.
- Mantuan allies can only include Bandellier Reiter and Infantry Regiments.

EARLY 17TH CENTURY FRENCH

Territory Types: Agricultural, Woodlands, Hilly

C-in-C	Great Commander/Field Commander/Troop Commander						80/50/35	1	
Sub-commanders	Field Commander						50	0–2	
	Troop Commander						35	0–3	

Troop name		Troop Type			Capabilities			Points per base	Bases per BG	Total bases
		Type	Armour	Quality	Shooting	Impact	Melee			
Core Troops										
Cuirassiers		Horse	Heavily Armoured	Superior	–	Pistol	Pistol	16	4	4–8
				Average				12		
Chevaux-légers or Carabins		Horse	Armoured	Average	–	Pistol	Pistol	10	4	4–12
		Horse	Unarmoured	Average	–	Pistol	Pistol	8	4	4–12
		Horse	Armoured	Average	Carbine	–	Pistol	11	4	
		Horse	Unarmoured	Average	Carbine	–	Pistol	9	4	
Forlorn hope Carabins		Light Horse	Unarmoured	Average	Carbine	–	Pistol	9	4	0–4
		Dragoons	Unarmoured	Average	Arquebus	–	–	7	4	
Veteran Guard infantry	Only before 1623	Medium Foot	Unarmoured	Superior	Arquebus	–	–	10	4	6	0–6
		Heavy Foot	Armoured	Superior	–	Pike	Pike	9	2	
	Only from 1623	Medium Foot	Unarmoured	Superior	Musket*	Impact Foot	–	11	4	6	0–12
		Heavy Foot	Armoured	Superior	–	Pike	Pike	9	2	
Other Guard, Vieux and Petits Vieux infantry	Only before 1623	Medium Foot	Unarmoured	Average	Arquebus	–	–	7	4	6	12–60
		Heavy Foot	Armoured	Average	–	Pike	Pike	6	2	
	Only from 1623	Medium Foot	Unarmoured	Average	Musket*	Impact Foot	–	8	4	6	
		Heavy Foot	Armoured	Average	–	Pike	Pike	6	2	
Field artillery		Medium Artillery	–	Average	Medium Artillery	–	–	20	2,3 or 4	2–4
		Light Artillery	–	Average	Light Artillery	–	–	12	2,3 or 4	
Optional Troops										
Enfants perdu	Only before 1623	Light Foot	Unarmoured	Average	Arquebus	–	–	6	4–6	0–8
Enfants perdu led by King's Musketeers	Only from 1623	Light Foot	Unarmoured	Average	Musket	–	–	7	4–6	
		Light Foot	Unarmoured	Superior	Musket	–	–	10	4	
Other French infantry and militia	Only before 1623	Medium Foot	Unarmoured	Poor	Arquebus	–	–	5	4	6	0–48
		Heavy Foot	Unarmoured	Poor	–	Pike	Pike	3	2	
	Only from 1623	Medium Foot	Unarmoured	Poor	Musket*	Impact Foot	–	6	4	6	
		Heavy Foot	Unarmoured	Poor	–	Pike	Pike	3	2	
Foreign infantry regiments		Medium Foot	Unarmoured	Average	Musket	–	–	8	4	6	0–18
		Heavy foot	Armoured	Average	–	Pike	Pike	6	2	
Allies										
Savoyard allies (only from 1625 to 1626) – Early Thirty Years' War German Catholic										
Mantuan allies (only from 1628 to 1631) – Early Thirty Years' War German Catholic										
Swedish allies (only in 1632) – Early Thirty Years' War Swedish										

EARLY 17TH CENTURY FRENCH ALLIES									
Allied commander		Field Commander/Troop Commander					40/25		1
Troop name		Troop Type			Capabilities		Points per base	Bases per BG	Total bases
		Type	Armour	Quality	Shooting	Impact	Melee		
Cuirassiers		Horse	Heavily Armoured	Superior	–	Pistol	Pistol	16	4	4
				Average				12		
Chevaux-légers or Carabins		Horse	Armoured	Average	–	Pistol	Pistol	10	4	4–8
		Horse	Unarmoured	Average	–	Pistol	Pistol	8	4	
		Horse	Armoured	Average	Carbine	–	Pistol	11	4	
		Horse	Unarmoured	Average	Carbine	–	Pistol	9	4	
Other Guard, Vieux and Petits Vieux infantry	Only before 1623	Medium Foot	Unarmoured	Average	Arquebus	–	–	7	4	6	6–24
		Heavy Foot	Armoured	Average	–	Pike	Pike	6	2	
	Only from 1623	Medium Foot	Unarmoured	Average	Musket*	Impact Foot	–	8	4	6
		Heavy Foot	Armoured	Average	–	Pike	Pike	6	2	
Artillery		Medium Artillery	–	Average	Medium Artillery	–	–	20	2	0–2

THIRTY YEARS' WAR DANISH

This list covers Danish armies from the start of the Swedish–Danish War in 1611 until the end of the Thirty Years' War.

During this period Denmark under Christian IV fought wars against Sweden in 1611–1613 (the Kalmar War) and 1643–1645, and intervened in the Thirty Years' War on the side of the Protestants from 1625 to 1629 – known as the *Kejserkrig* to the Danes, the war against the Emperor.

The Kalmar War was fought against Sweden with Christian's newly modernised and reformed army and was a success. The Swedish king, Gustavus Adolphus, was forced to give way on most of the Danish demands.

However, the subsequent wars were a different story. Despite usually being well equipped and supplied, the Danish army suffered defeats, resulting in Denmark being relegated to a second rank power in the Baltic, which was now dominated by their traditional enemies, the Swedes.

Danish pikemen

TROOP NOTES

During the Danish intervention in the Thirty Years' War Christian IV hired large numbers of German mercenaries partly paid with French and English gold. Those hired from territories close to Denmark were integrated into the army easily, but some groups hired from further away were less easily accommodated and are treated as an allied contingent.

THIRTY YEARS' WAR DANISH STARTER ARMY		
Commander-in-Chief	1	Field Commander
Sub-Commanders	2	2 x Troop Commander
Cuirassiers	2 BGs	Each comprising 4 bases of cuirassiers: Superior, Heavily Armoured, Horse – Impact Pistol, Melee Pistol
Arquebusiers	1 BG	4 bases of arquebusiers: Average, Armoured, Horse – Carbine, Melee Pistol
Infantry Regiments (LT)	2 BGs	Each comprising 9 bases of infantry regiments: 3 Average, Armoured, Heavy Foot – Pike; and 6 Average, Unarmoured, Medium Foot – Musket (Later Tercio)
Infantry Regiments	2 BGs	Each comprising 6 bases of infantry regiments: 2 Average, Armoured, Heavy Foot – Pike; and 4 Average, Unarmoured, Medium Foot – Musket
Marines	1 BG	4 bases of marines: Average, Armoured, Heavy Foot – Heavy Weapon
Dragoons	1 BG	3 bases of dragoons: Average, Unarmoured, Dragoons – Musket
Field Guns	1 BG	2 bases of field guns: Average Medium Artillery – Medium Artillery
Camp	1	Unfortified camp
Total	10 BGs	Camp, 12 mounted bases, 39 foot bases, 3 commanders

BUILDING A CUSTOMISED LIST USING OUR ARMY POINTS

Choose an army based on the maxima and minima in the list below. The following special instructions apply to this army:

- Commanders should be depicted as Cuirassiers.
- Battle groups designated as "(LT)" count as later tercios as defined in the rule book.

THIRTY YEARS' WAR DANISH

Territory Types: Agricultural

C-in-C	Great Commander/Field Commander/Troop Commander					80/50/35	1	
Sub-commanders	Field Commander					50	0–2	
	Troop Commander					35	0–3	

Troop name		Troop Type			Capabilities			Points per base	Bases per BG	Total bases
		Type	Armour	Quality	Shooting	Impact	Melee			
Core Troops										
Cuirassiers	Any date	Horse	Heavily Armoured	Superior	–	Pistol	Pistol	16	4	4–12
	Only from 1629	Horse	Armoured	Superior	–	Pistol	Pistol	13	4	
Arquebusiers		Horse	Armoured	Average	Carbine	–	Pistol	11	4–6	4–12
			Unarmoured					9		
Infantry regiments	Only before 1629	Medium Foot	Unarmoured	Average	Musket	–	–	8	6	9 (LT)
		Heavy Foot	Armoured	Average	–	Pike	Pike	6	3	9–90
	Only from 1625	Medium Foot	Unarmoured	Average	Musket	–	–	8	4	6
		Heavy Foot	Armoured	Average	–	Pike	Pike	6	2	
Field guns		Medium Artillery	–	Average	Medium Artillery	–	–	20	2, 3 or 4	2–4
Optional Troops										
Dragoons		Dragoons	Unarmoured	Average	Musket	–	–	8	2, 3 or 4	0–4
Marines		Heavy Foot	Armoured	Average	–	Heavy Weapon	Heavy Weapon	6	4–6	0–12
Heavy artillery		Heavy Artillery	–	Average	Heavy Artillery	–	–	25	2	0–2
Entrenchments and barricades		Field Fortifications	–	–	–	–	–	3	–	0–48
Allies										
German mercenary allies (1624–1626) – Early Thirty Years' War German Protestant										
Special Campaigns										
Only Danish intervention during the Thirty Years' War (1625 to 1629)										
German mercenary Kürassiere		Horse	Heavily Armoured	Superior	–	Pistol	Pistol	16	4	4–8
German mercenary Bandellier Reiter		Horse	Armoured	Average	Carbine	–	Pistol	11	4–6	0–12
			Unarmoured					9		
German mercenary foot		Medium Foot	Unarmoured	Average	Musket	–	–	8	4	6	12–48
		Heavy Foot	Armoured	Average	–	Pike	Pike	6	2	
			Unarmoured					5		

EARLY THIRTY YEARS' WAR GERMAN PROTESTANT

The Holy Roman Empire had never been a properly unified political construct and things had become worse after Luther had introduced religion as a further cause of division. Tension between the Catholic and Reformed Religions had been increasing since the late 16th century. A legally dubious move by the Emperor to allow the Catholic Maximilian I of Bavaria to punish the free city of Donauwörth (for breaking the religious peace by interfering with the Catholic minority practicing their beliefs) and the subsequent forcible re-Catholicisation of the city, finally convinced several Protestant leaders to form a defensive union in 1608. However, many Protestant leaders abstained from taking part, mostly because the Protestants themselves were split along Calvinist and Lutheran lines and the defence union was mostly led by Calvinists.

The attempt of the Archduke Ferdinand II to re-Catholicise economically important Bohemia

Bandellier reiter

led to the famous 2nd Defenestration of Prague in 1618, and a revolt of the Bohemians against the Emperor. The Palatine Elector Friedrich V used this to get himself elected King of Bohemia. In an attempt to limit the inevitable conflict, the Protestant Union agreed with the Emperor on an armistice that excluded Bohemia, thus isolating Friedrich V. Deprived of support and hoping vainly for help from England or the Low Countries, the initially promising revolt was now facing serious trouble. The only real help was a small mercenary army under Ernst von Mansfeld, and Bethlen Gábor's revolt and subsequent invasion of Hungary. While Bethlen's actions tied up Imperial troops the Emperor could still rely on the Catholic League and Spanish troops to carry out his war, ultimately leading to a total Bohemian defeat near Prague at the Battle of White Mountain (1620).

Whilst the fighting in Bohemia ended in May 1621, Friedrich V and other Protestant rulers attempted to regain the Rhenish Palatinate from the Spanish and the Catholic League until 1624. These efforts were supported by the Dutch, who had been battling the Spanish for decades, and who could not ignore a strong Spanish presence on the Rhine. Still Protestant attempts ended in defeat in almost every battle, most notably the battles of Wimpfen and Höchst in 1622.

The war might have ended here, but England, Denmark, the Lower Saxon Circle and the Dutch created the Protestant Coalition of the Hague, which planned to attack the Habsburgs on multiple fronts. However, the strongest member, Christian IV of Denmark, found foreign help from the coalition somewhat lacking. The Dutch and English only offered moral support, and co-ordination with the Protestant leaders of the other planned fronts, Christian von Braunschweig-Wolfenbüttel and Ernst von Mansfeld, proved difficult at best.

In the end Mansfeld was defeated by Wallenstein at the Battle of Dessau Bridge in April 1626, and in the same month Christian IV was also heavily defeated by Tilly at the Battle of Lutter. After his defeat at Dessau Bridge, Ernst von Mansfeld tried to link up with Bethlan Gábor, but Gábor had already been forced to sign a peace treaty with Friedrich II. So Mansfeld was stranded in the Balkans with his army and, lacking pay, his troops deserted him. Mansfeld himself died in late 1626.

Fearing Swedish intervention in Germany, Wallenstein persuaded Friedrich II to sign a generous peace treaty with Christian IV in June 1629. However, in the same year, Friedrich II also issued the highly controversial Edict of Restitution, which allowed Catholics to regain control of territories, churches, monasteries, etc. that had been under Protestant ownership since the second half of the 16th century. This gave Gustavus Adolphus, King of Sweden, a formal reason to start his invasion, which he did with a small force in summer 1630. Having secured a base of operation, and aided by French money, Gustavus quickly increased the size of his army, becoming a formidable force. Despite this, the Protestant powers of Germany were reluctant to directly assist him. In 1631, however, Johann Georg of Saxony's army joined Gustavus and together they met Tilly's combined League and Imperial army at the First Battle of Breitenfeld where, despite the Saxon army almost wholly routing on first contact, Tilly was overwhelmingly defeated.

This list covers German Protestant armies of the early Thirty Years' War from the start of the Bohemian revolt in 1618 to the First Battle of Breitenfeld (September 17, 1631).

EARLY THIRTY YEARS' WAR GERMAN PROTESTANT STARTER ARMY		
Commander-in-Chief	1	Field Commander
Sub-Commanders	2	2 x Troop Commander
Kürassiere	1 BG	4 bases of kürassiere: Superior, Heavily Armoured, Horse – Impact Pistol, Melee Pistol
Kürassiere	1 BG	4 bases of kürassiere: Average, Heavily Armoured, Horse – Impact Pistol, Melee Pistol
Bandellier Reiter	2 BGs	Each comprising 4 bases of bandellier reiter: Average, Unarmoured, Horse – Carbine, Melee Pistol
Foot regiments in larger formations (LT)	1 BG	9 bases of foot regiments in larger formations: 3 Average, Armoured, Heavy Foot – Pike; 6 Average, Unarmoured, Medium Foot – Musket (Later Tercio)
Other foot regiments	3 BGs	Each comprising 6 bases of other foot regiments: 2 Average, Armoured, Heavy Foot – Pike; and 4 Average, Unarmoured, Medium Foot – Musket
Dragoner	1 BG	3 bases of dragoons: Average, Unarmoured, Dragoons – Musket
Musketenkompanien	1 BG	4 bases of musketenkompanien: Average, Unarmoured, Medium Foot – Musket
Field guns	1 BG	2 bases of field guns: Average Medium Artillery – Medium Artillery
Camp	1	Unfortified camp
Total	11 BGs	Camp, 16 mounted bases, 36 foot bases, 3 commanders

EARLY THIRTY YEARS' WAR GERMAN PROTESTANT

German mercenary cavalry, 1632, by Richard Hook © Osprey Publishing Ltd. Taken from Men-at-Arms 262: The Army of Gustavus Adolphus (2): Cavalry.

TROOP NOTES

Many Protestant German infantry started the Thirty Years' War in regiments that were theoretically up to 3,000 men strong, but they deployed in bodies of around 1,000 men 10 ranks deep, with large regiments forming multiple bodies. We consider that these are best represented by the Later Tercio rules. However, at the same time, smaller units based on the Dutch model were coming into fashion and eventually supplanted the larger formations.

Ill-equipped foot are hastily raised regiments lacking training and proper equipment, like armour or good muskets. (In one extreme case there is even mention of about 1/3 of the shooters having to make do with crossbows.) We treat the mixture as arquebus and unarmoured pike to account for their reduced effectiveness. On the few occasions these regiments actually got into battle, they proved no more than a speed bump for the Catholic infantry. More usually they ran before being actually engaged.

Most Dutch infantry were incorporated into regular regiments. A few showed up as complete fighting units and were deployed in their native style. Regardless of organisation, Low Countries infantry in Germany was regularly considered to lack motivation and courage.

Ungarn were Hungarian hussars (though often recruited from Croatia and other non-Hungarian Slavic areas). They served in Protestant armies until Bethlen Gábor was forced to give up the Hungarian throne as part of the peace Treaty of Nikolsburg.

BUILDING A CUSTOMISED LIST USING OUR ARMY POINTS

Choose an army based on the maxima and minima in the list below. The following special instructions apply to this army:

- Commanders should be depicted as Kürassiere.
- No more than half of the Dutch infantry battle groups can be of Average quality.
- After 1626 at least half of the battle groups in the army must be of Poor quality.
- Battle groups designated "(LT)" count as later tercios as defined in the rule book.

EARLY THIRTY YEARS' WAR GERMAN PROTESTANT									
Territory Types: Agricultural, Hilly, Woodlands									
C-in-C	Great Commander/Field Commander/Troop Commander						80/50/35	1	
Sub-commanders	Field Commander						50	0–2	
	Troop Commander						35	0–3	
Troop name	Troop Type			Capabilities			Points per base	Bases per BG	Total bases
	Type	Armour	Quality	Shooting	Impact	Melee			
Core Troops									
Kürassiere	Any date	Horse	Heavily Armoured	Superior	–	Pistol	Pistol	16	4	0–16
		Horse	Heavily Armoured	Average	–	Pistol	Pistol	12	4	
	Only from 1626	Horse	Armoured	Superior	–	Pistol	Pistol	13	4	
		Horse	Armoured	Average	–	Pistol	Pistol	10	4	
Bandellier Reiter		Horse	Armoured	Average	Carbine	–	Pistol	11	4–6	8–24
			Unarmoured		Carbine	–		9		
			Armoured	Poor	Carbine	–	Pistol	8		
			Unarmoured		Carbine	–		7		
Foot regiments in larger formations	Only before 1626	Medium Foot	Unarmoured	Average	Musket	–	–	8	6	9 (LT)	18–66
		Heavy Foot	Armoured	Average	–	Pike	Pike	6	3	
Other foot regiments		Medium Foot	Unarmoured	Average	Musket	–	–	8	4	6	
		Heavy Foot	Armoured	Average	–	Pike	Pike	6	2	
		Medium Foot	Unarmoured	Poor	Musket	–	–	6	4	6	
		Heavy Foot	Armoured	Poor	–	Pike	Pike	4	2	
Ill-equipped foot		Medium Foot	Unarmoured	Poor	Arquebus	–	–	5	4	6	
		Heavy Foot	Unarmoured	Poor	–	Pike	Pike	3	2	
Field guns		Medium Artillery	–	Average	Medium Artillery	–	–	20	2, 3 or 4	2–4
			–	Poor	Medium Artillery	–	–	14		
Optional Troops									
Ungarn	Before 1622	Light Horse	Unarmoured	Average	Carbine	–	–	7	4–6	0–12
			Unarmoured	Average	Carbine	–	Pistol	9		
Dragoner		Dragoons	Unarmoured	Average	Musket	–	–	8	3 or 4	0–6
Bürgeraufgebot		Mob	Unarmoured	Poor	–	–	–	2	8–12	0–12
Musketenkompanien		Medium Foot	Unarmoured	Average	Musket	–	–	7	4–6	0–12
Dutch infantry		Medium Foot	Unarmoured	Average	Musket	–	–	8	4	6	0–24
		Heavy Foot	Armoured	Average	–	Pike	Pike	6	2	
		Medium Foot	Unarmoured	Poor	Musket	–	–	6	4	6	
		Heavy Foot	Armoured	Poor	–	Pike	Pike	4	2	
Heavy artillery		Heavy Artillery	–	Average	Heavy Artillery	–	–	25	2	0–2
Schanzen & barrikaden		Field Fortifications	–	–	–	–	–	3	–	0–48
Allies									
Transylvanian allies (before 1622) – Hungarian–Transylvanian									

EARLY THIRTY YEARS' WAR GERMAN PROTESTANT ALLIES

Allied commander			Field Commander/Troop Commander			40/25		1	
Troop name		**Troop Type**		**Capabilities**			**Points per base**	**Bases per BG**	**Total bases**
		Type	Armour	Quality	Shooting	Impact	Melee		
Kürassiere	Any date	Horse	Heavily Armoured	Superior	–	Pistol	Pistol	16	4	
		Horse	Heavily Armoured	Average	–	Pistol	Pistol	12	4	0–8
	Only from 1626	Horse	Armoured	Superior	–	Pistol	Pistol	13	4	
		Horse	Armoured	Average	–	Pistol	Pistol	10	4	
Bandellier Reiter		Horse	Armoured	Average	Carbine	–	Pistol	11	4–6	4–12
			Unarmoured					9		
			Armoured	Poor	Carbine	–	Pistol	8		
			Unarmoured					7		
Foot regiments in larger formations	Only before 1626	Medium Foot	Unarmoured	Average	Musket	–	–	8	6	9 (LT)
		Heavy Foot	Armoured	Average	–	Pike	Pike	6	3	
Other Foot regiments		Medium Foot	Unarmoured	Average	Musket	–	–	8	4	6
		Heavy Foot	Armour	Average	–	Pike	Pike	6	2	
		Medium Foot	Unarmoured	Poor	Musket	–	–	6	4	6
		Heavy Foot	Armoured	Poor	–	Pike	Pike	4	2	6–36
Ill equipped foot		Medium Foot	Unarmoured	Poor	Arquebus	–	–	5	4	6
		Heavy Foot	Armoured	Poor	–	Pike	Pike	3	2	
Field Guns		Medium Artillery	–	Average	Medium Artillery	–	–	20	2	0–2
				Poor				14		

EARLY THIRTY YEARS' WAR GERMAN CATHOLIC

As a reaction to the founding of the Protestant Union, the elector Maximilian I of Bavaria created the Catholic League. The League proved to be much more unified than the Protestant Union and its troops were entrusted to Johann t'Serclaes, Graf von Tilly, who went on to prove himself as probably the most capable general of his time.

After the outbreak of the Bohemian revolt and with the Imperial army weak and otherwise engaged, Maximilian offered the Emperor the services of the armed forces of the Catholic League – a move partly inspired by the latter's offer of the Electoral title held by Friedrich V to Maximilian.

Emperor Friedrich II accepted Maximilian's offer and in July 1620 30,000 League troops under Graf von Tilly moved into Austria, forcing the Austrian Estates to break their alliance with Bohemia. From Austria, Tilly marched into Bohemia, where he quickly won several victories until he managed to decisively defeat the Protestant army under Christian I von Anhalt at the Battle of White Mountain (1620). Supported by Spanish troops from the Low Countries, and despite a rare defeat by Ernst von Mansfeld at the battle of Wiesloch (1622), Tilly then went on to conquer the Rhineland palatinate.

Thus ended the first phase of the Thirty Years' War, but peace was not to be enjoyed, due to the formation of the Protestant Coalition of the Hague. However, Friedrich II was ahead of the coalition. As early as 1624 he had appointed a capable military leader who was directly answerable to the Emperor – Albrecht von Waldstein, better known as Wallenstein. This was necessary as Tilly was head of the Catholic League, which was answerable to Maximilian of Bavaria rather than the Emperor. If Maximilian should decide to pull out of the war, having achieved all his personal goals and becoming the only Elector with two votes, the Emperor might easily find himself with insufficient troops and without a reliable military leader. Wallenstein proved to be a good choice. In April 1625, he was created Generalissimo of all the Imperial troops. He went on to recruit some 24,000 troops to fight for the Emperor and was made the Duke of Friedland. He and Tilly made for a formidable combination, and the three-pronged attack planned by the coalition came to naught.

After shattering the armies of Christian von Braunschweig-Wolfenbüttel and Ernst von Mansfeld, the two Catholic generals then drove Christian IV back to Denmark. While Schleswig and Jutland were occupied by Tilly, Wallenstein occupied Mecklenburg. As a reward for this success, Friedrich II made Wallenstein Duke of Mecklenburg and named him "General of the whole Imperial Fleet and Lord of the Atlantic and Baltic". Wallenstein also invaded Pomerania, but failed to take the important city of Stralsund due to Danish and Swedish intervention. Another attack on Wallenstein's army by the Danes was routed with loss, but, fearing a Swedish intervention, Wallenstein persuaded Friedrich II to sign a generous peace treaty with Christian in June 1629.

Partly because of his success, Wallenstein was not well-liked by the electoral princes as, through him, a Holy Roman Emperor had, for the first time in decades, the power to enforce his will by military means. So when the time came for Friedrich II to ensure the continuity of his line on the throne (which required the electors to elect his son King of the Romans) the electoral princes jumped at the chance to pressure the Emperor to dismiss Wallenstein and cut the size of the Imperial army by two-thirds.

Unfortunately, about the same time, the Swedish King, Gustavus Adolphus, invaded Germany. With Wallenstein out of the way and the Imperial army reduced in size and engaged in northern Italy, Gustavus stormed from one victory to the next. Even the combined armies of the Catholic League and what Imperial troops were available, led by the renowned Tilly, failed to stop the Swedes at the First Battle of Breitenfeld. Tilly managed to rebuild an army but was defeated again at the Battle of Rain in April 1632. He subsequently died of wounds received there. With the Catholic cause in disarray, Wallenstein was reinstated by the Emperor and rapidly rebuilt his army.

This list covers German Imperial and Catholic League armies of the early Thirty Years' War from the start of the Bohemian revolt in 1618 until the death of Tilly in June 1632. It also includes the armies of Savoy that were involved in the minor conflicts in and around Italy, such as the War of the Mantuan Succession, 1628–1631.

Graf von Tilly

Imperial pikemen, 1618, by Darko Pavlovic © Osprey Publishing Ltd. Taken from Men-at-Arms 457:
Imperial Armies of the Thirty Years' War (1): Infantry and artillery.

TROOP NOTES

Regiments of the Catholic League, especially those of Bavarian origin, tended to be a lot larger than Imperial regiments. They commonly fielded about 2,000 to 2,500 men in actual fighting strength, whilst imperial regiments tended to have no more than 1,000 (although most were substantially larger on paper). Due to this, and Tilly's obsession with arranging his pikes in a somewhat old fashioned wide and deep formation based on the square root method, League infantry regiments can be fielded as Early Tercios. Other regiments formed up in smaller bodies and are therefore classified as Later Tercios.

Crabaten (Croats), Ungarn & Kossaken are collective terms for various light eastern type auxiliary riders of varying quality. At the start of the war they were mainly Polish Kossacks. After control of Hungary had passed back to the Habsburgs, the majority were Hungarian hussars (though these were commonly recruited in Croatia). They were found in substantial numbers mainly in Imperial armies, so should not be used for pure Catholic League armies.

Whilst ideally the Kürassiere were three-quarter armoured from head to knee, this was not always possible; some units fell below the standard and were closer to Bandellier Reiter in their equipment. Despite this, they still charged to contact and reserved their pistols for combat rather than shooting at longer range.

Tartshier were a development from the old Landsknecht forlorn hope troops and were equipped with armour and shield that were supposedly bullet proof, and swords. Their main role by this time was to disperse "unprotected" musketeers i.e. those not supported by pike. Montecuccoli also wanted them to front pike formations, but he admitted that this was unlikely to happen in practice.

Veteran infantryman

EARLY THIRTY YEARS' WAR GERMAN CATHOLIC STARTER ARMY		
Commander-in-Chief	1	Field Commander
Sub-Commanders	2	2 x Troop Commander
Kürassiere	2 BGs	Each comprising 4 bases of kürassiere: Superior, Heavily Armoured, Horse – Impact Pistol, Melee Pistol
Bandellier Reiter	1 BG	4 bases of bandellier reiter: Average, Armoured, Horse – Carbine, Melee Pistol
Infantry Regiments (LT)	3 BGs	Each comprising 9 bases of infantry regiments: 3 Average, Armoured, Heavy Foot – Pike; and 6 Average, Unarmoured, Medium Foot – Musket (Later Tercio)
Musketencompanien	1 BG	6 bases of musketencompanien: Average, Unarmoured, Medium Foot – Musket
Crabaten, Ungarn and Kossaken	1 BG	4 bases of crabaten, ungarn and kossaken: Average, Unarmoured, Light Horse – Carbine
Field artillery	1 BG	2 bases of field artillery: Average Medium Artillery – Medium Artillery
Camp	1	Unfortified camp
Total	9 BGs	Camp, 16 mounted bases, 35 foot bases, 3 commanders

BUILDING A CUSTOMISED LIST USING OUR ARMY POINTS

Choose an army based on the maxima and minima in the list below. The following special instructions apply to this army:

* Commanders should be depicted as Kürassiere.
* If Tilly's veterans are used, the C-in-C must be Johann t'Serclaes, Graf von Tilly (Johann Tserclaes, Count of Tilly), and be either a Great Commander or a Field Commander.
* Savoyard armies can only include Core Troops, a single battle group of Light Horse, Dragoons, Militia and Field Fortifications.
* Only one allied contingent may be fielded.
* Battle groups designated as "(ET)" and "(LT)" respectively count as early tercios and later tercios as defined in the rule book.

EARLY THIRTY YEARS' WAR GERMAN CATHOLIC									
Territory Types: Agricultural, Hilly, Woodlands									
C-in-C	Great Commander/Field Commander/Troop Commander						80/50/35	1	
Sub-commanders	Field Commander						50	0–2	
	Troop Commander						35	0–3	
Troop name		Troop Type			Capabilities		Points per base	Bases per BG	Total bases
		Type	Armour	Quality	Shooting	Impact	Melee		
Core Troops									
Kürassiere	Any date	Horse	Heavily Armoured	Elite	–	Pistol	Pistol	19	4	0–4	4–24
		Horse	Heavily Armoured	Superior	–	Pistol	Pistol	16	4	4–16
	Only from 1628	Horse	Armoured	Superior	–	Pistol	Pistol	13	4	0–12
Bandellier Reiter		Horse	Armoured	Average	Carbine	–	Pistol	11	4–6	0–12	4–18
			Unarmoured					9		4–18
Infantry regiments	Only Catholic League army	Medium Foot	Unarmoured	Average	Musket	–	–	8	6	12 (ET)	9–72
		Heavy Foot	Armoured	Average	–	Pike	Pike	6	6	
	Any	Medium Foot	Unarmoured	Average	Musket	–	–	8	6	9 (LT)
		Heavy Foot	Armoured	Average	–	Pike	Pike	6	3	
Field artillery		Medium Artillery	–	Average	Medium Artillery	–	–	20	2, 3 or 4	2–4
Optional Troops									
Tilly's veterans	Only Tilly's League army from 1622 to 1631	Medium Foot	Unarmoured	Superior	Musket	–	–	11	6	12 (ET)	0–36
		Heavy Foot	Armoured	Superior	–	Pike	Pike	9	6	
Other veteran infantry		Medium Foot	Unarmoured	Superior	Musket	–	–	11	6	9 (LT)	0–18
		Heavy Foot	Armoured	Superior	–	Pike	Pike	9	3	
Militia regiments	Any	Medium Foot	Unarmoured	Poor	Musket	–	–	6	6	9 (LT)	0–36
		Heavy Foot	Unarmoured	Poor	–	Pike	Pike	3	3	
Crabaten, Ungarn & Kossaken		Light Horse	Unarmoured	Average	Carbine	–	–	7	4–6	0–12
		Light Horse	Unarmoured	Average	Carbine	–	Pistol	9	4–6	
Dragoner		Dragoons	Unarmoured	Average	Musket	–	–	8	3 or 4	0–8
Schützenkompanien		Light Foot	Unarmoured	Superior	Musket	–	–	10	4	0–4

Musketenkompanien	Medium Foot	Unarmoured	Average	Musket	–	–	7	4–6	0–12
Tartschier	Heavy Foot or Medium Foot	Heavily Armoured	Superior	–	–	Swordsmen	10	4–6	0–6
Heavy artillery	Heavy Artillery	–	Average	Heavy Artillery	–	–	25	2	0–2
Schanzen & barrikaden	Field Fortifications	–	–	–	–	–	3	–	0–30
Allies									
Spanish allies (before 1626) – Later Imperial Spanish									
French allies (only Savoy 1625 to 1626) – Early 17th Century French									

Imperial musketeers, 1618, by Darko Pavlovic © Osprey Publishing Ltd. Taken from Men-at-Arms 457:
Imperial Armies of the Thirty Years' War (1): Infantry and artillery.

EARLY THIRTY YEARS' WAR GERMAN CATHOLIC ALLIES									
Allied commander		Great Commander/Field Commander/Troop Commander					80/50/35		1
Troop name		Troop Type			Capabilities		Points per base	Bases per BG	Total bases
		Type	Armour	Quality	Shooting	Impact	Melee		
Kürassiere	Any date	Horse	Heavily Armoured	Superior	–	Pistol	Pistol	16	4	4–12
	Only from 1628	Horse	Armoured	Superior	–	Pistol	Pistol	13	4	0–8	4–12
Bandellier Reiter		Horse	Armoured	Average	Carbine	–	Pistol	11	4–6	0–4	4–8
			Unarmoured					9		4–8
Infantry regiments	Only Catholic League army	Medium Foot	Unarmoured	Average	Musket	–	–	8	6	12 (ET)
		Heavy Foot	Armoured	Average	–	Pike	Pike	6	6	
	Any	Medium Foot	Unarmoured	Average	Musket	–	–	8	6	9 (LT)	9–36
		Heavy Foot	Armoured	Average	–	Pike	Pike	6	3	
Crabaten, Ungarn & Kossaken	Only Imperial	Light Horse	Unarmoured	Average	Carbine	–	–	7	4	0–4
		Light Horse	Unarmoured	Average	Carbine	–	Pistol	9	4	
Field artillery		Medium Artillery	–	Average	Medium Artillery	–	–	20	2	0–2

HUNGARIAN-TRANSYLVANIAN

This list covers the Hungarian-Transylvanian armies of Bethlen Gábor during the Thirty Years' War from 1618 – 1626, and also those of György I Rákóczi until the peace of Linz in December 1645.

Depending on the point of view, these wars were either an uprising against the Habsburg overlords or the actions of an independent (but Turkish supported) realm during the chaos that was the Thirty Years' War. Whilst these rulers were the Fürsten von Siebenbürgen (Dukes of Transylvania) many of their troops came from other parts of Hungary

Bethlen Gábor was a Calvinist nobleman from Transylvania who, thanks to Turkish assistance, won the title of Prince of Transylvania in 1613. Equally hostile to Austria and to the Ottoman Turks (but able to hide this very well), he sought to use both in order to create a united Hungary.

Whilst many of the common people in Hungary favoured him, large sections of the staunchly Roman Catholic Hungarian nobility rejected him.

In September 1619 Bethlen started his first major campaign against Habsburg Hungary, swiftly conquering most of Upper Hungary including Pressburg, modern day Bratislava, the key to Lower Austria. By October 1619 it looked as though Bethlen's army would join forces with the Bohemian Protestant army, which would have caused serious problems for the Catholic forces. However de Homonnay, an old enemy of Bethlen, had assembled a force in Poland and invaded Upper Hungary, obliging Bethlen to march back to defend it and thus probably saving Vienna.

In January 1620 Bethlen was "officially" crowned King of Hungary and immediately proclaimed religious tolerance throughout his realm. For the whole year Bethlen kept up small scale operations, securing additional parcels of territory for his Hungarian realm.

After his Bohemian allies suffered total defeat at the Battle of White Mountain in 1621, Bethlen ceased all further advances and tried to negotiate a peace treaty with Emperor Friedrich II, but was rejected. After several incursions into Lower Austria and taking parts of Moravia, Bethlen was finally able to coerce Friedrich II into peace talks, much to his relief as he was convinced that without additional aid from either Venice or the Turks he would not be able to keep going. The peace of Nikolsburg granted Bethlen the right to several counties in Hungary, but obliged him to renounce the Hungarian Crown and give up the recently conquered areas.

However, this peace wasn't to last long. Having secured support from the Turks, and believing the Protestants had the Imperial forces well occupied, Bethlen started a new offensive in mid 1623. Again he swiftly conquered large areas of Hungary and Moravia, and moved in on lower Austria. This time there was even a Turkish army ready to join forces with him. Before this came to pass, however, massive logistical problems, in part created by the Catholic Hungarian nobility, forced Bethlen to offer a truce (something Wallenstein had urged Friedrich to offer already) and fell back. By mid 1624 a new treaty had been signed, more or less reinstating the treaty of Nikolsburg.

A third attack by Bethlen in 1626 went along similar lines. He was militarily successful but unable to keep his army supplied without resorting to the same brutal foraging methods other Thirty Years' War armies employed. Thus Bethlen was again forced to sue for peace. The treaty of Pressburg again restated the terms of Nikolsburg.

In the end Bethlen had failed to create a united Hungary, but succeeded in preserving the political and territorial integrity of Transylvania for years to come. What set Bethlen apart were his diplomatic skills and economically sound politics. The former allowed him to get comparably generous peace terms every time even although he had broken former treaties, and the latter permitted him to actually sustain his army without relying on plunder and foraging as much as other armies did during the Thirty Years' War.

After Bethlen's death his younger brother Istvan followed him on the throne, but abdicated after just two months, freeing the way for György I Rákóczi. While György favoured a very aggressive anti-Habsburg policy, he lacked the many talents of Bethlen, and as a result also lacked the money and troops. So for almost 18 years he was just a nuisance to the Habsburgs. While he undertook regular large scale raids into Habsburg Hungary, these had very little lasting effect and only served to make him unpopular with the Hungarian people. Only in 1643, after he agreed to treaties first with the Swedes and shortly after also with France, did he receive the economic backing and experienced military advisors needed to conduct a large scale invasion into Hungary. During the next two years he managed to occupy most of Hungary. Just before he could take Pressburg, and combine his forces with the Swedish army under Lennart Torstensson, political pressure by the Ottomans forced him to abandon further military action.

TROOP NOTES

Bethlen's Transylvanian and Hungarian troops were frequently veterans with considerable combat experience, but were mostly used to

Szekler

fighting Turkish border troops in a style of warfare consisting of skirmishes, raids and counter-raids. Owing to the nature of the fighting in the area, the heavy infantry that had become the mainstay in the rest of Europe was rare and not very good. Hence Bethlen found it necessary to supplement his native troops with mercenary infantry. Additionally he lacked sufficient artillery by the standards of the day.

The nature of the warfare that Transylvania was involved in allowed traditional lancers to survive far longer in this area than in other neighbouring countries. They appear to have still formed the core of the heavy cavalry in Bethlen's army in 1619 & 1620. Whilst over time they adopted pistols in addition to their other weapons, they still maintained an aggressive charging attack as their usual doctrine. For defence they wore "Trabharnische" – basically 3/4 plate armour – at the start of this period. This style of armour was considered outdated by the end of the 16th century in western Europe. One theory for its survival in

this area (aside of Hungary-Transylvania just being somewhat of a backwater) is that such armour was effective against the arrows of the Turks thus saving the horseman – although their unprotected horses would still suffer badly. Over time, and with more exposure to the western way of war one assumes, they changed to the somewhat less complete, but stronger around vital areas, armour of the German Cuirassiers. Those that couldn't afford the more complete armour found themselves among the Viteji or Hussars.

Dorobanti are Wallachian and Transylvanian mercenaries using muskets and large axes. We classify them as Musket*, Heavy Weapon.

Haiduks were border settlers and highly skilled at guerrilla type warfare. Classification of Szekler foot is problematic as we know very little about them, but they generally seem to have fought in a similar style to the Haiduks, so we group them together.

Peasants armed with arquebus fought in support of Bethlen's mercenary infantry.

HUNGARIAN-TRANSYLVANIAN STARTER ARMY		
Commander-in-Chief	1	Field Commander
Sub-Commanders	2	2 x Troop Commander
Boyars	1 BG	4 bases of boyars: Superior, Heavily Armoured, Gendarmes – Light Lancers, Melee Pistol
Viteji	1 BG	4 bases of viteji: Average, Unarmoured, Horse – Carbine, Melee Pistol
Hussars	1 BG	4 bases of hussars: Average, Unarmoured, Cavalry – Carbine, Melee Pistol
Hussars	3 BGs	Each comprising 4 bases of hussars: Average, Unarmoured, Light Horse – Bow, Swordsmen
Hussars	1 BG	4 bases of hussars: Average, Unarmoured, Light Horse – Bow
Szekler or veteran Hussars	1 BG	4 bases of szekler or veteran Hussars: Superior, Unarmoured, Cavalry – Bow, Swordsmen
Seimeni	1 BG	3 bases of seimeni: Average, Unarmoured, Dragoons – Musket
Dorobanti	1 BG	6 bases of dorobanti: Average, Unarmoured, Heavy Foot – Musket*, Heavy Weapon
Haiduks	1 BG	6 bases of haiduks: Superior, Unarmoured, Medium Foot – Musket, Swordsmen
Camp	1	Unfortified camp
Total	11 BGs	Camp, 32 mounted bases, 15 foot bases, 3 commanders

BUILDING A CUSTOMISED LIST USING OUR ARMY POINTS

Choose an army based on the maxima and minima in the list below. The following special instructions apply to this army:

- Commanders should be depicted as Boyars.
- Battle groups designated as "(LT)" count as later tercios as defined in the rule book.

HUNGARIAN-TRANSYLVANIAN									
Territory Types: Agricultural, Hilly, Woodlands									
C-in-C	Great Commander/Field Commander/Troop Commander						80/50/35		1
Sub-commanders	Field Commander						50		0–2
	Troop Commander						35		0–3
Troop name	Troop Type			Capabilities			Points per base	Bases per BG	Total bases
	Type	Armour	Quality	Shooting	Impact	Melee			
Core Troops									
Boyars	Only before 1629	Gendarmes	Heavily Armoured	Superior	–	Heavy Lancers	Swordsmen	21	4–6	4–12 before 1621 0–8 from 1621
	Any date	Gendarmes	Heavily Armoured	Superior	–	Light Lancers	Pistol	21	4–6	0–8 before 1621
		Cavaliers	Armoured	Superior	–	Light Lancers	Pistol	19	4–6	4–12 from 1621
Viteji		Horse	Armoured	Average	Carbine	–	Pistol	11	4–6	4–12
			Unarmoured					9		
Hussars		Cavalry	Unarmoured	Average	Carbine	–	Pistol	10	4–6	8–40
					Bow	–	Swordsmen	10		
		Light Horse	Unarmoured	Average	Bow	–	Swordsmen	9		
					Carbine	–	Pistol	9		
		Light Horse	Unarmoured	Average	Bow	–	–	7	4–6	0–12
					Carbine	–	–	7		
Szekler or veteran Hussars		Cavalry	Unarmoured	Superior	Carbine	–	Pistol	13	4–6	4–16
					Bow	–	Swordsmen	13		
			Armoured	Superior	Carbine	–	Pistol	16		
					Bow	–	Swordsmen	16		
		Light Horse	Unarmoured	Superior	Carbine	–	Pistol	12		
					Bow	–	Swordsmen	12		
Optional Troops									
Seimeni		Dragoons	Unarmoured	Average	Musket	–	–	8	3 or 4	0–8
Dorobanti		Heavy Foot	Unarmoured	Average	Musket*	Heavy Weapon	Heavy Weapon	7	6–8	0–12
			Armoured					8		
Haiduks or Szekler Foot		Light Foot	Unarmoured	Average	Musket	–	–	7	6–8	0–18
				Superior				10		0–6
		Medium Foot	Unarmoured	Superior	Musket	Swordsmen		11	6–8	0–12
				Average				7		
Peasants armed with arquebus'	Only before 1627	Medium Foot	Unarmoured	Poor	Arquebus	–	–	4	6–12	0–12
Peasants		Mob	Unarmoured	Poor	–	–	–	2	8–12	0–12
Mercenary Arquebusiers		Horse	Armoured	Average	Carbine	–	Pistol	11	4	0–8
			Unarmoured					9		

Mercenary Cuirassiers	Only before 1635	Horse	Heavily Armoured	Superior	–	Pistol	Pistol	16	4	
				Average				12		0–8
Mercenary demi-cuirassiers	Only from 1635	Horse	Armoured	Average	–	Pistol	Pistol	10	4	
Mercenary Infantry	Only before 1627	Medium Foot	Unarmoured	Average	Musket	–	–	8	6	9 (LT)
		Heavy Foot	Armoured	Average	–	Pike	Pike	6	3	
	Any date	Medium Foot	Unarmoured	Average	Musket	–	–	8	4	6
		Heavy Foot	Armoured	Average	–	Pike	Pike	6	2	0–27
Field Guns		Medium Artillery	–	Average	Medium Artillery	–	–	20	2	0–2

HUNGARIAN–TRANSYLVANIAN ALLIES										
Allied commander		Field Commander/Troop Commander						40/25		1
Troop name		Troop Type			Capabilities			Points per base	Bases per BG	Total bases
		Type	Armour	Quality	Shooting	Impact	Melee			
Boyars	Only before 1629	Gendarmes	Heavily Armoured	Superior	–	Heavy Lancers	Swordsmen	21	4–6	4–8 before 1621 / 0–4 from 1621
	Any date	Gendarmes	Heavily Armoured	Superior	–	Light Lancers	Pistol	21	4–6	0–4 before 1621
		Cavaliers	Armoured	Superior	–	Light Lancers	Pistol	19	4–6	4–8 from 1621
Viteji		Horse	Armoured	Average	Carbine	–	Pistol	11	4–6	0–6
			Unarmoured					9		
Hussars		Cavalry	Unarmoured	Average	Carbine	–	Pistol	10	4–6	4–20
					Bow	–	Swordsmen	10		
		Light Horse	Unarmoured	Average	Bow	–	Swordsmen	9	4–6	0–6
					Carbine	–	Pistol	9		
			Unarmoured	Average	Bow	–	–	7		
					Carbine	–	–	7		
Szekler or veteran Hussars		Cavalry	Unarmoured	Superior	Carbine	–	Pistol	13	4–6	4–8
					Bow	–	Swordsmen	13		
			Armoured	Superior	Carbine	–	Pistol	16		
					Bow	–	Swordsmen	16		
		Light Horse	Unarmoured	Superior	Carbine	–	Pistol	12		
					Bow	–	Swordsmen	12		

EARLY CAROLINE ENGLISH

*U*nlike his father James I (of England, VI of Scotland), Charles I was romantic and somewhat impetuous. He was thus willing to involve England in foreign wars, which were universally unsuccessful.

His first foreign expedition was against Spain, with an attack on Cádiz in 1625. Whilst his Parliament was willing to fund a naval expedition, Charles wished to send an army, which resulted in a poorly supplied force being landed under the command of Sir Edward Cecil. Despite Cecil being an experienced soldier (he had seen extensive service in Dutch pay) he had no experience of naval expeditions, which resulted in the army being landed in the wrong place without enough food or water. When the hungry and thirsty soldiers found a supply of wine, nearly the whole army was reduced to drunkenness. Cecil decided the situation was hopeless. Abandoning the expedition, he re-embarked the army, although the Spanish captured 1,000 men who were still drunk.

Despite this disaster, Charles again sent an expedition overseas in 1627, this time to France. Charles's favourite, the Duke of Buckingham, was in command, and the aim was to aid the French Huguenots. This expedition landed on the Île de Ré in an attempt to capture the town of Saint-Martin. As with Cádiz, the expedition was badly supplied and the attempt was a failure. The army had to be re-embarked and withdrawn. In 1628 two attempts were made to send reinforcements to La Rochelle, but both were dismal failures, with the English forces having no effect at all. La Rochelle was forced to surrender.

Following this embarrassment, Charles realised that England was in no position to effectively intervene on the Continent, and no further expeditions were sent abroad during the period Charles ruled without calling a Parliament. Despite

this, by the late 1630s Charles had managed to stir up religious controversy in England and Scotland. By trying to enforce a new prayer book on his Scottish kingdom, he caused them to rebel against him under the aegis of the "Solemn League and Covenant" which led to the two "Bishops' Wars". As with his earlier military adventures, both of these were disasters for Charles. Although there was no fighting in the first war, in the second a Scottish army invaded England, defeating Charles' army at the Battle of Newburn and capturing Newcastle, thus forcing Charles into a humiliating peace.

If trouble with his Scottish subjects was not enough, his Catholic Irish subjects then raised a rebellion in 1641, leading to a war that lasted until 1652 when the rebellion was finally crushed by the army of the English Commonwealth.

This list covers the pre-Civil War English armies of the reign of Charles I, including the overseas expeditions to Spain and France and the two Bishops' Wars of 1639 and 1640. It also includes various armies in Ireland from 1634, when the army was organised by Viscount Wentworth, through its partial disbandment on his impeachment, reinforcement on the outbreak of the Irish rebellion in 1641, and fragmentation following the cessation of 1643 which allowed some troops to be sent to fight for the king in England.

EARLY CAROLINE ENGLISH STARTER ARMY		
Commander-in-Chief	1	Field Commander
Sub-Commanders	2	2 x Troop Commander
Horse	2 BGs	Each comprising 4 bases of horse: Average, Armoured, Horse – Carbine, Melee Pistol
Horse	1 BG	4 bases of horse: Average, Unarmoured, Horse – Carbine, Melee Pistol
Cuirassiers	1 BG	4 bases of cuirassiers: Average, Heavily Armoured, Horse – Impact Pistol, Melee Pistol
Foot	6 BGs	Each comprising 6 bases of foot: 2 Average, Armoured, Heavy Foot – Pike; and 4 Average, Unarmoured, Medium Foot – Musket*
Dragoons	1 BG	3 bases of dragoons: Average, Unarmoured, Dragoons – Musket
Medium Artillery	1 BG	2 bases of medium artillery: Average Medium Artillery – Medium Artillery
Camp	1	Unfortified camp
Total	12 BGs	Camp, 16 mounted bases, 41 foot bases, 3 commanders

TROOP NOTES

A unit of cuirassiers was raised in Ireland at the time of the Bishops' Wars for service in England – there is no evidence of it serving in Ireland. At this time English cavalry were using "Harquebusier" tactics and later, in the First English Civil War, Haselrigge's "Lobsters" at Roundway Down may have received a Royalist charge halted – which possibly indicates that English cuirassiers did not charge in the way their continental counterparts would. However, we give them the benefit of the doubt and allow them the option of Pistol Impact Phase capability.

Despite the existence of theoretically well equipped and at least partly drilled "Trained Band" militia, Charles instead chose to raise forces for the Bishops' Wars by commission. These forces proved to be badly equipped and poorly motivated, and some northern levies are stated to have actually turned up armed with bills and longbows instead of pikes and muskets. The horse, however, proved to be somewhat better and performed acceptably, although they were beaten at Newburn.

BUILDING A CUSTOMISED LIST USING OUR ARMY POINTS

Choose an army based on the maxima and minima in the list below. The following special instructions apply to this army:

- Commanders should be depicted as Cuirassiers or Horse.
- Only one Cuirassier battle group can be used.
- Armies in Ireland cannot have more than four battle groups of mounted troops, all of which must be Unarmoured.
- The minimum marked * only applies after 1629 or if any mounted troops are fielded. This represents the wholly infantry armies sent to Spain and France.

Cuirassier

EARLY CAROLINE ENGLISH

Territory Types: Agricultural, Hilly, Woodlands

C-in-C	Great Commander/Field Commander/Troop Commander				80/50/35	1	
Sub-commanders	Field Commander				50	0–2	
	Troop Commander				35	0–3	

Troop name		Troop Type			Capabilities			Points per base	Bases per BG	Total bases
		Type	Armour	Quality	Shooting	Impact	Melee			
Core Troops										
Horse		Horse	Armoured	Average	Carbine	–	Pistol	11	4	*8–24
				Poor				8		
			Unarmoured	Average	Carbine	–	Pistol	9	4	
				Poor				7		
Foot	Any outside Ireland	Medium Foot	Unarmoured	Average	Musket*	–	–	7	4	6	24–144
		Heavy Foot	Armoured	Average	–	Pike	Pike	6	2	
	Only in Ireland from 1634 to 1643	Medium Foot	Unarmoured	Average	Musket	–	–	8	4	6	24–96
		Heavy Foot	Unarmoured	Average	–	Pike	Pike	5	2	
		Medium Foot	Unarmoured	Poor	Musket*	–	–	5	4	6	0–48
		Heavy Foot	Unarmoured	Poor	–	Pike	Pike	3	2	
Heavy artillery		Heavy Artillery	–	Average	Heavy Artillery	–	–	25	2	0–2	0–4
Medium artillery		Medium Artillery	–	Average	Medium Artillery	–	–	20	2, 3 or 4	0–4
Optional Troops										
Cuirassiers		Horse	Heavily Armoured	Average	–	Pistol	Pistol	12	2 or 4	0–4
					Carbine	–	Pistol	13		
Dragoons	Only before 1634	Dragoons	Unarmoured	Average	Arquebus	–	–	7	2, 3 or 4	0–4
	Only from 1634	Dragoons	Unarmoured	Average	Musket	–	–	8	2, 3 or 4	
Special Campaigns										
Only Bishops' Wars 1639 and 1640										
Replace Foot with poorly equipped and motivated levies		Medium Foot	Unarmoured	Poor	Musket*	–	–	5	4	6	All
		Heavy Foot	Unarmoured	Poor	–	Pike	Pike	3	2	
Replace Dragoons with poorly equipped and motivated troops		Dragoons	Unarmoured	Poor	Arquebus	–	–	5	2, 3 or 4	All
Ill equipped northern levies		Medium Foot	Unarmoured	Poor	Bow*	–	–	3	4	6	0–12
		Heavy Foot	Unarmoured	Poor	–	Heavy Weapon	Heavy Weapon	3	2	
Sconces and other earthworks		Field Fortifications	–	–	–	–	–	3	–	0–10

EARLY CAROLINE ENGLISH ALLIES									
Allied commander	Field Commander/Troop Commander						40/25	1	
Troop name	Troop Type			Capabilities			Points per base	Bases per BG	Total bases
	Type	Armour	Quality	Shooting	Impact	Melee			
Horse	Horse	Unarmoured	Average	Carbine	–	Pistol	9	4	0–8
			Poor				7		
Foot	Medium Foot	Unarmoured	Average	Musket*	–	–	7	4	12–48
	Heavy Foot	Armoured	Average	–	Pike	Pike	6	2	6
Medium artillery	Medium Artillery	–	Average	Medium Artillery	–	–	20	2	0–2

EARLY THIRTY YEARS' WAR SWEDISH

Sweden had long desired to break the Danish domination of the Baltic Sea, and one part of Gustavus Adolphus' plan to manage this was for Sweden to obtain a foothold on the German Baltic coast of Pomerania. Having brought his latest war with Poland to an end in 1629 with the generally favourable Truce of Altmark, Gustavus was free to intervene in the Thirty Years' War. On 6th July 1630 Swedish troops arrived at Usedom, off Pomerania, to join 5,000 men already at Stralsund, and the build up continued slowly over the course of the year. To reinforce his ability to wage a war in Germany, Sweden being a poor country, Gustavus concluded an alliance with France, which provided him with a cash subsidy of 400,000 talers annually.

Despite his arrival at a low point for the Protestant cause in the war, and his stated aim, whether true or not, of restoring "German liberties", there was little immediate support for Gustavus. It took a combination of the Edict of Restitution, the sack of Magdeburg and the Emperor authorising Tilly to demand supplies from Saxony to force the reluctant Elector of Saxony, Johann Georg, to join the Swedes, bringing with him a well equipped army of 18,000 men.

Gustavus and Johann Georg met Tilly in battle in September 1631. Despite the Saxon army fleeing from the field at the first clash, the well drilled and confident Swedish army went on to completely defeat Tilly's League army. The most significant result of the battle was that it finally decided the minds of German Protestants, who now flocked to Gustavus' banner. This was vital as Sweden was too small to provide the necessary manpower for an extended war in Germany, and was too poor to finance it. German soldiers, raised by German officers, were an absolute necessity.

Following Breitenfeld the Swedes and their German allies proceeded to advance into southern Germany, carrying all before them. Tilly was killed in early 1632 and the Emperor was forced to recall Wallenstein, whom he had previously sacked at the insistence of the Imperial Princes. 1632 saw the King and Wallenstein campaigning over large areas of Germany, with the King desperate to force a major battle and, hopefully, destroy the Imperial army, setting the stage for him to dictate terms to the Emperor. His eagerness for battle caused the King to attempt a foolish attack on Wallenstein when he was heavily entrenched at Alte Veste, where failure cost him many men. Later in the year, however, his chance came as he caught Wallenstein at Lützen when Wallenstein had started to disperse his army into winter quarters. The resulting battle was long, confused and bloody, with the Swedes once again attacking the Imperial army in a well chosen position. At the end of the day both Gustavus and the inspirational Imperial cavalry general, Papenheim, were dead, and the cream of the Swedish infantry had been shattered. However, Wallenstein had also lost heavily and chose to withdraw under cover of darkness, which allowed the Swedes to claim victory as they held the field.

The death of Gustavus was a serious blow to the Swedes and they were somewhat paralysed by his loss. Politically the chancellor, Oxenstierna, now led Sweden, but who was to lead the army was less clear. In the end the Swedish marshal, and Oxenstierna's son-in-law, Gustav Horn, and the German prince, Bernhard von Sachsen-Weimar, took command of the army, having to put down a mutiny caused by lack of pay as one of their first acts.

Despite the loss of Gustavus, the war continued to go well for the Swedes and their allies. This was helped by the murder of Wallenstein in early 1634. However, much as with Breitenfeld, the whole situation was to be turned on its head by a single battle, Nördlingen. Here the armies of Horn and Sachsen-Weimar foolishly attacked the combined forces of the Emperor and the Spanish Cardinal-Infante who were well entrenched in a good position. Another bloody battle ensued, resulting in the almost complete destruction of the infantry of the Swedish armies in repeated brave, but futile, attacks on the veteran Spanish tercios brought from Italy.

Gustavus Adolphus and Swedish cavalry at Lützen, 1632, by Richard Hook © Osprey Publishing Ltd. Taken from Men-at-Arms 262: The Army of Gustavus Adolphus (2): Cavalry.

Swedish cavalry

is the first definitive evidence that this formation depth was being used in Germany by the Swedes, who had deployed deeper in their wars against the Poles. It is, however, unclear if this was a recent change or more established, and so we optionally allow such formations (as represented by the Determined Horse classification) for the whole period of this list.

The Finnish cavalry, known as *Hakkapeliita* from their war cry of *"hakkaa päälle!"* (hack them down), were better mounted and had a fearsome reputation for savagery and brutality. They were the best of Gustavus' cavalry and at Lützen he turned to them to attack the Imperial cuirassiers who were the greatest threat – *"charge me those blacke fellows soundly: for they are the men who will undo us"*. There is some uncertainty about how well equipped the Finns were. Certainly at times they were not equipped to the standard required of the Swedish cavalry, but this may not have been the case for the troops in Germany. Both interpretations are allowed for.

Long service German mercenary cavalry adopted Swedish tactics, however, we assume that more recently recruited units may have at least initially retained their traditional tactics.

Inevitably, the cavalry were better placed to escape, but for the time being the Swedes had no field army in being.

This list covers the Swedish armies in Germany during the so called "Swedish phase" of the Thirty Years' War, from Gustavus' landing in 1630 until the first battle of Nördlingen in 1634.

TROOP NOTES

Up to the first battle of Breitenfeld in 1631, the Swedish native cavalry was poorly horsed and so cannot be rated above Average, despite their undoubted good morale. Following the decisive defeat of Tilly's army at this battle, and the flood of support from German Protestants thereafter, better mounts became available in significant numbers and were allocated to the native cavalry, sometimes to the detriment of the German units. Even then this was no guarantee that the cavalry would do well; one account from the Battle of Lützen in 1632 states: *"Had not our foote stoode like a wall, there had not a man of us come off alive … our horse did but poorely"*.

The Swedish and German cavalry at the Battle of Lützen are shown as being deployed 3 ranks deep, unlike the Imperialists who are 6 deep. This

Swedish infantry with regimental gun

The Yellow Regiment at Lützen 1632, by Richard Hook © Osprey Publishing Ltd. Taken from Men-at-Arms 235: The Army of Gustavus Adolphus (1): Infantry.

EARLY THIRTY YEARS' WAR SWEDISH STARTER ARMY		
Commander-in-Chief	1	Field Commander
Sub-Commanders	2	2 x Troop Commander
Swedish lätta ryttare and veteran German cavalry	2 BGs	Each comprising 4 bases of Swedish lätta rytarre or veteran German cavalry: Average, Armoured, Determined Horse – Impact Pistol, Melee Pistol
Mercenary karbinryttare	1 BG	4 bases of mercenary karbinryttare: Average, Unarmoured, Horse – Carbine, Melee Pistol
Veteran "colour regiments"	1 BG	7 bases of veteran "colour regiments": 3 Superior, Armoured, Heavy Foot – Pike; 4 Superior, Unarmoured, Medium Foot – Salvo; and 1 Superior Regimental Guns (deployed in Swedish brigade)
Other regiments	2 BGs	Each comprising 7 bases of other regiments: 3 Average, Armoured, Heavy Foot – Pike; 4 Average, Unarmoured, Medium Foot – Salvo; and 1 Average Regimental Guns (deployed in Swedish brigade)
Mercenary infantry regiments	1 BG	6 bases of mercenary infantry regiments: 2 Average, Armoured, Heavy Foot – Pike; and 4 Average, Unarmoured, Medium Foot – Musket
Commanded shot	1 BG	2 bases of commanded shot: Average, Unarmoured, Medium Foot – Salvo; and 1 Average Regimental Guns
12-pounder guns	1 BG	2 bases of 12-pounder guns: Average, Medium Artillery – Medium Artillery
Camp	1	Unfortified camp
Total	9 BGs	Camp, 12 mounted bases, 31 foot bases, 3 commanders

BUILDING A CUSTOMISED LIST USING OUR ARMY POINTS

Choose an army based on the maxima and minima in the list below. The following special instructions apply to this army:

- Commanders should be depicted as lätta ryttare, with or without armour. Gustavus should never be depicted in armour, however.

- At least half the Swedish brigade battle groups must have regimental guns.
- If any Commanded Shot battle groups have regimental guns then all must.
- Saxon allies in 1631 cannot have more than one Average infantry battle group.
- Only one allied contingent may be fielded.

EARLY THIRTY YEARS' WAR SWEDISH									
Territory Types: Agricultural, Woodlands, Hilly									
C-in-C	Great Commander/Field Commander/Troop Commander						80/50/35		1
Sub-commanders	Field Commander						50		0–2
	Troop Commander						35		0–3
Troop name	Troop Type			Capabilities			Points per base	Bases per BG	Total bases
	Type	Armour	Quality	Shooting	Impact	Melee			
Core Troops									
Swedish *lätta ryttare* and veteran German cavalry	Only before 1633	Horse	Armoured	Average	–	Pistol	Pistol	10	4	4–24
	Any date	Determined Horse	Armoured	Average	–	Pistol	Pistol	15	4	
	Only from 1632	Determined Horse	Armoured	Superior	–	Pistol	Pistol	21	4	
Finnish *hakkapeliita*		Cavaliers	Armoured	Elite	–	Impact Mounted	Pistols	24	4	0–4
				Superior				21		
		Cavaliers	Unarmoured	Elite	–	Impact Mounted	Swordsmen	21	4	
				Superior				18		
Mercenary *karbinryttare*		Horse	Armoured	Average	Carbine	–	Pistol	11	4–6	4–16
			Unarmoured					9		
Commanded shot		Medium Foot	Unarmoured	Superior	Salvo	Salvo	–	11	2	2–8
				Average				8		
Infantry deployed in Swedish brigades	Only Yellow brigade before 1633	Medium Foot	Unarmoured	Elite	Salvo	Salvo	–	13 +4	4 7	0–7	7–70
		Heavy Foot	Armoured	Elite	–	Pike	Pike	11	3	
	Veteran "colour regiments"	Medium Foot	Unarmoured	Superior	Salvo	Salvo	–	11 +4	4 7	7–28
		Heavy Foot	Armoured	Superior	–	Pike	Pike	9	3	
	Other regiments	Medium Foot	Unarmoured	Average	Salvo	Salvo	–	8 +4	4 7	0–70
		Heavy Foot	Armoured	Average	–	Pike	Pike	6	3	
3-pounder guns attached to Swedish brigades		Regimental Guns	–	Elite	Regimental Guns	Regimental Guns	–	14	n/a	0–1 per Swedish brigade BG
				Superior				12		
				Average				9		
12-pounder guns		Medium Artillery	–	Average	Medium Artillery	–	–	20	2, 3 or 4	2–6
24-pounder guns		Heavy Artillery	–	Average	Heavy Artillery	–	–	25	2, 3 or 4	

Optional Troops										
Dragoons and mounted jägers		Dragoons	Unarmoured	Average	Musket	–	–	8	3 or 4	0–6
German or Livonian cuirassiers		Horse	Heavily Armoured	Superior	–	Pistol	Pistol	16	4	0–4
3-pounder guns attached to commanded shot	Only from 1632	Regimental Guns	–	Superior	Regimental Guns	Regimental Guns	–	12	n/a	0 or 1 per commanded shot BG
				Average				9		
Mercenary infantry regiments	Only from 1633	Medium Foot	Unarmoured	Average	Musket	–	–	8	4	6	0–36
		Heavy Foot	Armoured	Average	–	Pike	Pike	6	2		

Allies
Saxon, Hessen – Kassel or other German Protestant allies – Early Thirty Years' War German Protestant (only in 1631) or Later Thirty Years' War German (only from 1632)
French allies (only in 1632) – Early 17th Century French

EARLY THIRTY YEARS' WAR SWEDISH ALLIES

Allied commander		Field Commander/Troop Commander						40/25		1
Troop name		**Troop Type**			**Capabilities**			**Points per base**	**Bases per BG**	**Total bases**
		Type	Armour	Quality	Shooting	Impact	Melee			
Swedish *lätta ryttare* and veteran German cavalry	Only before 1633	Horse	Armoured	Average	–	Pistol	Pistol	10	4	4–8
	Any date	Determined Horse	Armoured	Average	–	Pistol	Pistol	15	4	
	Only from 1632	Determined Horse	Armoured	Superior	–	Pistol	Pistol	21	4	
Mercenary *karbinryttare*		Horse	Armoured	Average	Carbine	–	Pistol	11	4–6	0–8
			Unarmoured					9		
Commanded shot		Medium Foot	Unarmoured	Superior	Salvo	Salvo	–	11	2	0–4
				Average				8		
Infantry deployed in Swedish brigades	Veteran "colour regiments"	Medium Foot	Unarmoured	Superior	Salvo	Salvo	–	11	4	7	0–7	7–35
		Heavy Foot	Armoured	Superior	–	Pike	Pike	9	+4	3		
	Other regiments	Medium Foot	Unarmoured	Average	Salvo	Salvo	–	8	4	7	7–35	
		Heavy Foot	Armoured	Average	–	Pike	Pike	6	+4	3		
3-pounder guns attached to Swedish brigades		Regimental Guns	–	Superior	Regimental Guns	Regimental Guns	–	12	n/a	0–1 per Swedish brigade BG
				Average				9		
12-pounder guns		Medium Artillery	–	Average	Medium Artillery	–	–	20	2	0–2

LATER THIRTY YEARS' WAR GERMAN

*T*he *First Battle of Breitenfeld* had transformed the military situation in Germany. After this battle no army stood in the way of Gustavus Adolphus, as Wallenstein was still busy rebuilding his forces. The situation was desperate enough that Ferdinand considered withdrawing the Edict of Restitution and fleeing to Italy. By May 1632, Augsburg and Munich had fallen to Gustavus, who was now at the height of his power. However, his future campaigns were less successful.

Avoiding an immediate direct confrontation, Wallenstein moved to Nuremberg, entrenching himself in a very strong position at the Alte Vetse. In September 1632, Gustavus launched an attack on the Alte Veste that failed miserably, leading to many mercenaries deserting the Swedish force. Wallenstein then marched north to Saxony. Gustavus found himself powerless to stop him as

The battle of Lützen, 1632 © Osprey Publishing Ltd. Taken from Essential Histories 29: The Thirty Years' War 1618–1648.

Wallenstein captured Leipzig and then moved to camp his army at Lützen for the winter.

Here on November 16th 1632 the Battle of Lützen was fought. The surprise attack Gustavus had attempted turned out not to be a surprise, and in fact Wallenstein had succeeded in drawing Gustavus out into a full-scale battle on his terms. The resulting battle was confused and bloody, but in the end Wallenstein chose to retreat and fell back into Bohemia. The Swedes claimed victory as they held the field, but at best this was a Pyrrhic victory, they having lost, amongst their many casualties, their charismatic King. Without him the Protestant forces now lacked direction. Count Horn and Bernhard von Sachsen-Weimar tried to take over the Protestant forces, but they lacked the authority of the late King.

Axel Oxenstierna, the regent for Gustavus' daughter, called for a meeting of Sweden, the Lower Saxon Circle and Saxony. The result was a defensive alliance, the Heilbronn League, whose stated goal was to defend Protestantism in north Germany. However, as the Saxon elector switched to supporting the Emperor, the new league basically became a puppet of France and Sweden. In November 1633, the forces of this "defensive" league had its first victory when it invaded Bavaria and captured Regensburg.

At the same time there was growing disquiet about Wallenstein within Imperialist ranks, not only at the court in Vienna, but also within his army. It is difficult to account for Wallenstein's actions. He was ill with gout and depression, and this may have affected his decisions. He may also have been playing a very complex strategy game which no-one else understood. The upshot of this was that in early 1634 Ferdinand ordered Wallenstein's arrest.

This order was made redundant when he was murdered by some of his officers in February 1634.

The command of the Imperial army was now given to Ferdinand, the son of the Emperor. He was married to the Spanish Infanta, bringing both houses of the Habsburgs closer together. Ferdinand (the son) also shared a friendship with the brother of his wife, the Spanish Cardinal-Infante Don Fernando. Both were able military leaders dedicated to turning back the tide of Protestantism that swept through Europe, and their friendship re-vitalized the Austrian-Spanish alliance.

The Imperial and Spanish armies joined forces in September 1634 near Nördlingen. They were opposed by the Protestant army under Horn and Bernhard, who had planned to break them up and defeat each army on its own. Since that plan failed, the outcome was a disaster for the Swedes, who were heavily defeated and Horn was captured. With this one great victory, the power of the Emperor was suddenly restored. The Heilbronn League was in total disarray. The Protestants had no army to speak of any more, while the Catholics now had two powerful armies again. It was almost a reversal of the situation after Breitenfeld. By the Spring of 1635, all Swedish resistance in the south of Germany had been extinguished. A peace process which had been started in 1634 ended with the Peace of Prague in May 1635, which took most of the Protestant powers in German out of the war.

This alarmed France, who, ever fearful of a strong and seemingly united Holy Roman Empire, but lacking the means to conduct a successful war herself, signed a treaty with Sweden in order to continue the fighting.

Bernhard von Sachsen-Weimar, commanding what was left of the Swedish army (now mainly Germans) could not attack without French support, but the French Rhine army had been held back near Lorraine, so Bernhard was forced to retreat and the Imperials took Kaiserslautern, Heidelberg and besieged Mainz. When Bernard was finally joined by the French in late July 1635, this allowed him to temporarily lift the siege of Mainz. With his army sadly diminished afterwards, Bernhard was then compelled to fall back to Metz. As a result, Mainz fell to Imperial forces in December 1635.

1636 saw a partial reverse in fortunes as Bernhard and La Valette made themselves the masters of almost all of Upper Alsace, and in October 1636 an Imperial army was defeated by the Swedes at Wittstock, allowing the occupation most of north Germany. Matthias Gallas and his army had to be recalled from the so far rather successful French campaign to confront the Swedes. The Battle of Torgau saw the defeat of the Swedish army and forced them back to Pomerania. Only the financial support of France allowed them to stay in the war at all.

In February 1637, the Emperor Ferdinand died and his son succeeded him as Ferdinand III.

In late 1637 Bernhard fought two bloody battles against Imperial armies. Although he lost the first, by winning at the second he was now in a position to break Imperial power along the Rhine by taking the key fortress of Breisach. The siege of the fortress began in June 1638, but only after receiving further French reinforcement was he strong enough to do so in earnest. Meanwhile two Imperial armies, under the Bavarian General Götz and the Imperial general Savello, were sent out together with a convoy of reinforcements for Breisach. They failed to join forces and

Kürassiere

allowed themselves to be defeated in detail by Bernhard who had been waiting for them.

By 1638 the Swedes had also realised that they needed to use more than just German mercenaries to fight their war, and had recruited reinforcements of over 14,000 men in Sweden. However, plans for a joint Franco–Swedish campaign in 1639 came to naught when Bernhard contracted the plague and died that summer. After some discussion, his colonels determined to serve their paymasters the French, and entered into an agreement under which the troops were to continue as a separate army in the service of France. Meanwhile the Swedes, having hoped in vain for the appearance of a French force, turned towards Saxony and swept through it, defeating the Imperials under Ferdinand's brother, the Archduke Leopold-Wilhelm, at Chemintz in April 1639.

With the problems around Bernhard over, the French and Swedes renewed their plans for a joint campaign. However, despite a powerful force being assembled in 1640, the results were less than impressive. The Imperial forces, now under Piccolomini, wisely refused battle. The Swedish commander, Banér, did not press the issue, and drifted aimlessly through central Germany toward the Weser. In the end, nothing was accomplished. A second campaign, involving the armies of Sweden, France and Brunswick, again accomplished nothing, with Banér spending all his energies quarrelling with the French commander, de Guebriant. Upon his return from the central German campaign, Banér fell sick and died in May 1641. His army, whose discipline had always been problematic at best, started to mutiny.

In July 1641, Brandenburg and Sweden signed a truce. Many other German princes followed Brandenburg's example to indicate their displeasure with Ferdinand III. In 1642, a Swedish army defeated an Imperial army at the Second Battle of Breitenfeld. In 1645, the Imperial army faced two defeats, at Nördlingen by the French, and Jankau by the Swedes. By now it had become clear that the Holy Roman Empire was no longer in a position to continue the war. On the other hand, its opponents were too weak to actually defeat it. Later in the same year, Sweden and Saxony signed a peace agreement, which meant that by 1646 Ferdinand III could no longer expect support from Saxony, Brandenburg or Spain.

Finally, in 1647, Maximilian of Bavaria was forced by the Swedes and French to withdraw his support to Ferdinand. When he broke this agreement in 1648, Swedish and French forces devastated Bavaria, leaving Maximilian no choice but to sign a truce. Bereft of all support, Ferdinand III finally agreed to the Peace of Westphalia, ending the Thirty Years' War.

This list covers German armies of the later Thirty Years' War from May 1632 to the end of the war in 1648.

TROOP NOTES

After the Swedish intervention, armies across Germany adopted formations that were similar to, if not exactly the same as, the Swedish ones. The infantry abandoned deep formations very quickly, in fact many had already done so by the start of this list, but the cavalry held onto older formations for longer.

In the aftermath of the Battle of Lützen, Wallenstein noted that the "unarmoured" cavalry (the Bandellier Reiter of this list) were the ones who had fled, whilst the armoured cavalry had stood and fought. He therefore ordered that all the cavalry be armoured and took away carbines from those that had them. However, this was not completed by the time of his assassination in 1634, and some troops carried on in the old style throughout the war.

LATER THIRTY YEARS' WAR GERMAN

Imperial pikemen, 1640, by Darko Pavlovic © Osprey Publishing Ltd. Taken from Men-at-Arms 457: Imperial Armies of the Thirty Years' War (1): Infantry and artillery.

Whilst German armies never adopted the Swedish brigade system (and in fact the Swedes themselves abandoned it around 1635 in the aftermath of the Battle of Nördlingen) regimental guns did become a feature, at least for a while.

As with most other armies of the period, armour was discarded as the campaigns wore on, especially amongst the infantry. However, the innate conservative nature of the Imperial armies meant that some regiments may have been issued with armour long after contemporaries had abandoned the practice. Veteran infantry, on the other hand, would have discarded the armour regardless. Whilst it is somewhat arbitrary, the aftermath of the Battle of Nördlingen has been taken as a cut off point, as major battles became less frequent after this, with armies just marching across Germany much of the time – an occupation that would discourage armour wearing.

Crabaten (Croats), Ungarn & Kossaken are collective terms for various light eastern type auxiliary riders of varying quality. They were found in substantial numbers mainly in Imperial armies.

LATER THIRTY YEARS' WAR GERMAN STARTER ARMY		
Commander-in-Chief	1	Field Commander
Sub-Commanders	2	2 x Troop Commander
Kürassiere	1 BG	4 bases of Kürassiere: Superior, Heavily Armoured Horse – Impact Pistol, Melee Pistol
Kürassiere	1 BG	4 bases of Kürassiere: Superior, Armoured Horse – Impact Pistol, Melee Pistol
Bandellier Reiter	1 BG	4 bases of Bandellier Reiter: Average, Unarmoured, Horse – Carbine, Melee Pistol
Infantry regiments	2 BGs	Each comprising 6 bases of infantry regiments: 2 Average, Armoured, Heavy Foot – Pike; and 4 Average, Unarmoured, Medium Foot
Infantry regiments	1 BG	6 bases of infantry regiments: 2 Average, Armoured, Heavy Foot – Pike; and 4 Average, Unarmoured, Medium Foot – Musket; and 1 Average Regimental Gun
Veteran infantry regiments	1 BG	6 bases of infantry regiments: 2 Superior, Armoured, Heavy Foot – Pike; and 4 Superior, Unarmoured, Medium Foot – Musket; and 1 Superior Regimental Gun
Commanded shot	1 BG	2 bases of commanded shot: 2 Average, Unarmoured, Medium Foot – Musket
Dragoner	1 BG	3 bases of dragoons: Average, Unarmoured, Dragoons – Musket
Crabaten, Ungarn & Kossaken	1 BG	4 bases of ungarn: Average, Unarmoured, Light Horse – Carbine
Field guns	1 BG	2 bases of field guns: Average Medium Artillery – Medium Artillery
Camp	1	Unfortified camp
Total	11 BGs	Camp, 16 mounted bases, 31 foot bases, 3 commanders

BUILDING A CUSTOMISED LIST USING OUR ARMY POINTS

Choose an army based on the maxima and minima in the list below. The following special instructions apply to this army:

- Commanders should be depicted as Kürassiere.
- Armies must be, nominally at least, either Catholic or Protestant.

- Protestant armies cannot use more than one battle group of Light Horse.
- Other than Catholic Imperial armies, Armoured pike cannot be used from 1635. Catholic Imperial armies cannot have more than half of their infantry regiments with Armoured pike.
- No more than one allied contingent can be used.

LATER THIRTY YEARS' WAR GERMAN									
Territory Types: Agricultural, Hilly, Woodlands									
C-in-C	Great Commander/Field Commander/Troop Commander						80/50/35	1	
Sub-commanders	Field Commander						50	0–2	
	Troop Commander						35	0–3	
Troop name	Troop Type			Capabilities			Points per base	Bases per BG	Total bases
	Type	Armour	Quality	Shooting	Impact	Melee			
Core Troops									
Kürassiere	Only before 1635	Horse	Heavily Armoured	Superior	–	Pistol	Pistol	16	4	0–16	4–24
	Only from 1635 to 1638	Horse	Heavily Armoured	Superior	–	Pistol	Pistol	16	4	0–8	
	Any date	Horse	Armoured	Superior	–	Pistol	Pistol	13	4	0–24	
		Horse	Armoured	Average	–	Pistol	Pistol	10	4		
	Only from 1635	Determined Horse	Armoured	Superior	–	Pistol	Pistol	21	4	0–16	
			Unarmoured					18			
		Determined Horse	Armoured	Average	–	Pistol	Pistol	15	4		
			Unarmoured					12			
Bandellier Reiter	Only before 1635	Horse	Armoured	Average	Carbine	–	Pistol	11	4–6	4–18
		Horse	Armoured	Poor	Carbine	–	Pistol	8	4–6	
		Horse	Unarmoured	Average	Carbine	–	Pistol	9	4–6	
		Horse	Unarmoured	Poor	Carbine	–	Pistol	7	4–6	
Dragoner		Dragoons	Unarmoured	Average	Musket	–	–	8	3 or 4	3–8
Infantry regiments	Any date	Medium Foot	Unarmoured	Average	Musket	–	–	8	4	6	12–60
		Heavy Foot	Armoured	Average	–	Pike	Pike	6	2		
	Only from 1635	Medium Foot	Unarmoured	Average	Musket	–	–	8	4	6	
		Heavy Foot	Unarmoured	Average	–	Pike	Pike	5	2		
Falkone		Regimental Guns	–	Average	Regimental Guns	Regimental Guns	–	9	n/a	0–1 per 2 Infantry Regiments
Light artillery		Light Artillery	–	Average	Light Artillery	–	–	12	2	2–6
Field guns		Medium Artillery	–	Average	Medium Artillery	–	–	20	2, 3 or 4	
Optional Troops									
Bandellier Reiter	Only from 1635	Horse	Unarmoured	Average	Carbine	–	Pistol	9	4	0–12
		Horse	Unarmoured	Poor	Carbine	–	Pistol	7	4	
Veteran infantry regiments	Only before 1635	Medium Foot	Unarmoured	Superior	Musket	–	–	11	4	6	0–18
		Heavy Foot	Armoured	Superior	–	Pike	Pike	9	2		
	Only from 1635	Medium Foot	Unarmoured	Superior	Musket	–	–	11	4	6	
		Heavy Foot	Unarmoured	Superior	–	Pike	Pike	8	2		
Falkone		Regimental Guns	–	Superior	Regimental Guns	Regimental Guns	–	12	n/a	0 or 1 per Veteran Infantry Regiment
Poor quality infantry regiments		Medium Foot	Unarmoured	Poor	Musket	–	–	6	4	6	0–24
		Heavy Foot	Unarmoured	Poor	–	Pike	Pike	3	2		

Troop name		Type	Armour	Quality	Shooting	Impact	Melee	Points per base	Bases per BG	Total bases
Commanded shot		Medium Foot	Unarmoured	Average	Musket	–	–	8	2	0–6
Crabaten, Ungarn & Kossaken		Light Horse	Unarmoured	Average	Carbine	–	–	7	4–6	0–12
		Light Horse	Unarmoured	Average	Carbine	–	Pistol	9		
Schützenkompanien		Light Foot	Unarmoured	Superior	Musket	–	–	10	4	0–4
Tartschier	Only Imperial before 1639	Heavy Foot or Medium Foot	Heavily Armoured	Superior	–	–	Swordsmen	10	4–6	0–6
				Average				7		
Heavy artillery		Heavy Artillery	–	Average	Heavy Artillery	–	–	25	2	0–2
Schanzen & barrikaden		Field Fortifications						3	–	0–30
Allies										

Spanish allies (only Catholics before 1640) – Later Imperial Spanish

Dutch allies (only Protestants) – Later Eighty Years' War Dutch

French allies (only Protestants or Savoy from 1637) – Early 17th Century French (before 1635) or Thirty Years' War French (from 1635)

Swedish allies (only Protestants) – Early Thirty Years' War Swedish (before 1635) or Later Thirty Years' War Swedish and Weimarian (from 1635)

LATER THIRTY YEARS' WAR GERMAN ALLIES

Allied commander		Field Commander/Troop Commander						40/25	1	
Troop name		**Troop Type**			**Capabilities**			**Points per base**	**Bases per BG**	**Total bases**
		Type	Armour	Quality	Shooting	Impact	Melee			
Kürassiere	Only before 1635	Horse	Heavily Armoured	Superior	–	Pistol	Pistol	16	4	0–8
	Only from 1635 to 1638	Horse	Heavily Armoured	Superior	–	Pistol	Pistol	16	4	0–4	4–12
	Any date	Horse	Armoured	Superior	–	Pistol	Pistol	13	4	0–12
		Horse	Armoured	Average	–	Pistol	Pistol	10	4	
	Only from 1635	Determined Horse	Armoured	Superior	–	Pistol	Pistol	21	4	0–8
			Unarmoured					18		
		Determined Horse	Armoured	Average	–	Pistol	Pistol	15	4	
			Unarmoured					12		
Bandellier Reiter	Only before 1635	Horse	Armoured	Average	Carbine	–	Pistol	11	4–6	4–8
		Horse	Armoured	Poor	Carbine	–	Pistol	8	4–6	
		Horse	Unarmoured	Average	Carbine	–	Pistol	9	4–6	
		Horse	Unarmoured	Poor	Carbine	–	Pistol	7	4–6	
Dragoner		Dragoons	Unarmoured	Average	Musket	–	–	8	2, 3 or 4	0–4
Infantry regiments	Any date	Medium Foot	Unarmoured	Average	Musket	–	–	8	4	6	6–30
		Heavy Foot	Armoured	Average	–	Pike	Pike	6	2	
	Only from 1635	Medium Foot	Unarmoured	Average	Musket	–	–	8	4	6
		Heavy Foot	Unarmoured	Average	–	Pike	Pike	5	2	
Falkone		Regimental Guns	–	Average	Regimental Guns	Regimental Guns	–	9	n/a	0–1 per 2 Infantry Regiments
Light artillery		Light Artillery	–	Average	Light Artillery	–	–	12	2	0–2
Field guns		Medium Artillery	–	Average	Medium Artillery	–	–	20	2	

The Imperial retreat, 1632, by Graham Turner © Osprey Publishing Ltd. Taken from Campaign 68: Lützen 1632.

LATER THIRTY YEARS' WAR SWEDISH AND WEIMARIAN

This list covers Swedish armies from the aftermath of the first battle of Nördlingen in 1634 until the Treaty of Westphalia in 1648 brought the Thirty Years' War to an end. It also includes the mercenary army of Bernhard von Sachsen-Weimar (the Weimarians or Bernhardines) in the service of France from 1635 until his death in 1639, and then its continued existence as the French *Armee d'Allemagne* until it became effectively just a normal French army (albeit with a significant German proportion) in 1644 following catastrophic losses in late 1643.

Following the catastrophic defeat at Nördlingen, the Swedes were forced back into northern Germany, desperately trying to recruit a replacement army with which to defend their Pomeranian possessions. Their situation was made worse as the Emperor agreed the Peace of Prague with the major Protestant powers, one clause of which was the delayed implementation of the Edict of Restitution for 40 years, which effectively meant it was a dead letter. At a stroke German support for Sweden was almost entirely removed. This act, as it significantly bolstered the Habsburg position, effectively forced France into the war.

As France was lacking an experienced army, and general, Richelieu negotiated a deal with Bernhard by which he would provide an army for France in exchange for massive French subsidies, along the lines of those previously paid to Gustavus. At the same time he was also the general of the Heilbronn League of minor German princes, which led him to veer between a French inspired policy and a Heilbronn inspired one, making him a somewhat erratic person to deal with. However, as he had an army in being, and was able to keep it at a meaningful strength most of the time, he could not be discarded. On his death from plague in 1639 his officers concluded a deal with Richelieu whereby their army more formally transferred into the service of France. From then on it was usually led by a French marshal, the most famous of whom was Turenne, who continued to lead the remaining Bernhardine units after their severe losses in 1643 forced the French to formally take the army into their establishment.

The Swedes, after consolidating their Pomeranian possessions and receiving reinforcements from home, again started to campaign to the south. For the next decade the war became one of attrition, with neither side able to deliver a knockout blow to the other. Armies marched vast distances to and fro across Germany which led to cavalry becoming the most important arm. However, this also resulted in the armies becoming smaller as horses need a lot of food and water to keep them in the field. When pitched battles did occur both sides had their successes, but in general the Swedes won more than they lost and towards the end of the 1640s their French allies were also becoming more effective. This led to a series of combined operations, with the French fighting in southern Germany and the Swedes further north, in order to defeat both the Bavarian led Catholic League and the Imperial armies. Eventually this proved successful, with Bavaria being forced out of the war in 1647. Facing total exhaustion and collapse, the Imperials finally agreed to peace in 1648, the famous Peace of Westphalia, which allowed a drastic reduction in armies across the whole of Germany.

TROOP NOTES

With the war now consisting of frequent long marches and fewer major engagements, armour became increasingly unpopular amongst the troops, who now routinely abandoned it as cumbersome and uncomfortable. At Christmas 1635 the Swedish chancellor Oxenstierna wrote *"No horsemen's or soldier's harness or pots need be sent here, since they have become little used, but mostly cast off because of the long marches one is engaged in here."* However, as Montecuccoli writing about 1640

Army arrayed for battle

at least implies that Swedish cavalry (like other demi-cuirassiers) wore armour, it would appear that it came back into use, thus Armoured classification is allowed from 1640.

The defeat at Nördlingen all but destroyed the veteran Swedish and German infantry regiments of the two main Swedish armies. Their replacements no longer used the Swedish brigade system and the associated salvo shooting, instead using the same formations and tactics as most other foot of the time. With the emphasis on marching, some regiments appear to have discarded their pikes as well as their armour. It was not until major Swedish foot levies were sent to Germany in 1638 that the Swedish element was again significant.

Whilst Commanded Shot were still used, this was no longer an automatic choice, as the cavalry was now at least as good as their enemies', and commanders often preferred to allow them full manoeuvrability rather than slow them down with attached infantry.

LATER THIRTY YEARS' WAR SWEDISH AND WEIMARIAN STARTER ARMY		
Commander-in-Chief	1	Field Commander
Sub-Commanders	2	2 x Troop Commander
Swedish and German "demi-cuirassiers"	2 BGs	Each comprising 4 bases of Swedish and German demi-cuirassiers: Superior, Unarmoured, Determined Horse – Impact Pistol, Melee Pistol
Swedish and German "demi-cuirassiers"	2 BGs	Each comprising 4 bases of Swedish and German demi-cuirassiers: Average, Unarmoured, Determined Horse – Impact Pistol, Melee Pistol
German or Swedish Infantry regiments	1 BG	6 bases of German or Swedish Infantry regiments: 2 Superior, Unarmoured, Heavy Foot – Pike; 4 Superior, Unarmoured, Medium Foot – Musket; and 1 Superior Battalion Guns – Regimental Guns
German or Swedish Infantry regiments	2 BGs	Each comprising 6 bases of German or Swedish Infantry regiments: 2 Average, Unarmoured, Heavy Foot – Pike; 4 Average, Unarmoured, Medium Foot – Musket
Commanded shot	1 BG	2 bases of commanded shot: Average, Unarmoured, Medium Foot – Musket
Dragoons	1 BG	3 bases of dragoons: Average, Unarmoured Dragoons – Musket
12-pounder guns	1 BG	2 bases of 12-pounder guns: Average, Medium Artillery – Medium Artillery
Camp	1	Unfortified camp
Total	10 BGs	Camp, 16 mounted bases, 25 foot bases, 3 commanders

BUILDING A CUSTOMISED LIST USING OUR ARMY POINTS

Choose an army based on the maxima and minima in the list below. The following special instructions apply to this army:

- Commanders should be depicted as demi-cuirassiers.

- Minima marked * only apply if any non-allied foot are used other than Musket only German infantry regiments and/or commanded shot.
- No more than half the Infantry Regiments fielded can be Superior.
- German and French allies may be fielded together, otherwise only one allied contingent may be fielded.

Swedish infantry, 1635, by Richard Hook © Osprey Publishing Ltd. Taken from Men-at-Arms 235:
The Army of Gustavus Adolphus (1): Infantry.

LATER THIRTY YEARS' WAR SWEDISH AND WEIMARIAN

Territory Types: Agricultural, Woodlands, Hilly									
C-in-C		Great Commander/Field Commander/Troop Commander					80/50/35		1
Sub-commanders		Field Commander					50		0–2
		Troop Commander					35		0–3

Troop name		Troop Type			Capabilities			Points per base	Bases per BG	Total bases
		Type	Armour	Quality	Shooting	Impact	Melee			
Core Troops										
Swedish and German "demi-cuirassiers"	Any date	Determined Horse	Unarmoured	Superior	–	Pistol	Pistol	18	4	8–40
				Average				12		
	Only from 1640	Determined Horse	Armoured	Superior	–	Pistol	Pistol	21	4	
				Average				15		
Dragoons		Dragoons	Unarmoured	Average	Musket	–	–	8	3 or 4	3–8
German or Swedish Infantry regiments		Medium Foot	Unarmoured	Superior	Musket	–	–	11	4	6	0–18	*12–48
		Heavy Foot	Unarmoured	Superior	–	Pike	Pike	8	2		
		Medium Foot	Unarmoured	Average	Musket	–	–	8	4	6	12–48
		Heavy Foot	Unarmoured	Average	–	Pike	Pike	5	2		
		Medium Foot	Unarmoured	Poor	Musket	–	–	6	4	6	0–24
		Heavy Foot	Unarmoured	Poor	–	Pike	Pike	3	2		
		Medium Foot	Unarmoured	Superior	Musket	–	–	10	6	0–12
				Average				7		
French Infantry Regiments	Only Weimarians from 1637	Medium Foot	Unarmoured	Average	Musket*	Impact Foot	–	8	4	6	0–24
		Heavy Foot	Unarmoured	Average	–	Pike	Pike	5	2		
Battalion guns		Regimental Guns	–	Superior	Regimental Guns	Regimental Guns	–	12	n/a	0–1 per non-Poor Infantry Regiment
				Average				9		
Light artillery		Light Artillery	–	Average	Light Artillery	–	–	12	2	*2–4
Field artillery		Medium Artillery	–	Average	Medium Artillery	–	–	20	2, 3 or 4	
Optional Troops										
Commanded shot		Medium Foot	Unarmoured	Average	Musket	–	–	8	2	0–8
Mercenary *Bandellier* Reiter		Horse	Unarmoured	Average	Carbine	–	Pistol	9	4	0–8
				Poor				7		
Allies										
German Protestant allies – Later Thirty Years' War German										
French allies – Thirty Years' War French										
Transylvanian allies (only in 1644) – Hungarian–Transylvanian										

LATER THIRTY YEARS' WAR SWEDISH AND WEIMARIAN ALLIES									
Allied commander		Field Commander/Troop Commander						40/25	1
Troop name		Troop Type			Capabilities			Points per base	Bases per BG	Total bases
		Type	Armour	Quality	Shooting	Impact	Melee			
Swedish and German "demi-cirassiers"	Any date	Determined Horse	Unarmoured	Superior	–	Pistol	Pistol	18	4	4–16
				Average				12		
	Only from 1640	Determined Horse	Armoured	Superior	–	Pistol	Pistol	21	4	
				Average				15		
Dragoons		Dragoons	Unarmoured	Average	Musket	–	–	8	2, 3 or 4	0–4
German or Swedish Infantry regiments		Medium Foot	Unarmoured	Superior	Musket	–	–	11	4	6	0–6
		Heavy Foot	Unarmoured	Superior	–	Pike	Pike	8	2		
		Medium Foot	Unarmoured	Average	Musket	–	–	8	4	6	6–24
		Heavy Foot	Unarmoured	Average	–	Pike	Pike	5	2		
		Medium Foot	Unarmoured	Poor	Musket	–	–	6	4	6	0–12	*6–24
		Heavy Foot	Unarmoured	Poor	–	Pike	Pike	3	2		
French Infantry Regiments	Only Weimarians from 1637	Medium Foot	Unarmoured	Superior	Musket	–	–	10	6	0–6
				Average		–	–	7		
		Medium Foot	Unarmoured	Average	Musket*	Impact Foot	–	8	4	6	0–12
		Heavy Foot	Unarmoured	Average	–	Pike	Pike	5	2		
Battalion guns		Regimental Guns	–	Superior	Regimental Guns	Regimental Guns	–	12	n/a	0–1 per non-Poor Infantry Regiment
				Average				9		
Light artillery		Light Artillery	–	Average	Light Artillery	–	–	12	2	0–2
Field artillery		Medium Artillery	–	Average	Medium Artillery	–	–	20	2	

THIRTY YEARS' WAR FRENCH

ollowing the Battle of Nördlingen in 1634, the French government, led by Cardinal Richelieu, was faced by the prospect of Habsburg domination of Germany and the Low Countries in addition to the southern border with Habsburg Spain. France would be surrounded by Habsburgs, who would then dominate the whole of Europe. This was obviously unacceptable, and France finally entered the Thirty Years' War proper in 1635 with a quaintly outdated formal declaration of war with Spain sent by herald to Brussels.

On paper France had formidable military resources and could deploy large numbers of men on multiple fronts. However, the reality was that these armies were inexperienced, especially compared to the Spanish, and there were, initially, few generals of any real skill. This, unsurprisingly, led to poor performance on the battlefield and a number of heavy defeats. 1636 was an especially bad year, the so called "Year of Corbie", when it was quite possible that Paris itself could have fallen to the

Cardinal-Infante. This was, however, weathered with some difficulty.

In this early stage of France's involvement, its only really effective army was the mercenary German army of Bernhard von Sachsen-Weimar operating within Germany on the Rhine.

With most of France's war now taking place on its own soil, there were additional financial hardships to be faced by the people. Richelieu had banked on the war being fought outside of France, where the armies could be billeted and obtain supplies from the local, enemy, populations, as was the norm in the Thirty Years' War, and so remove this burden from the state. As this proved impossible, in addition to the manpower needed to keep the armies up to strength, large sums of money were needed to pay them and Bernhard's army, which could only be obtained by additional taxation and loans.

Despite the heavy financial burden, the French managed to maintain armies on three or more fronts simultaneously, including opening a southern theatre of war by invading Spain itself to draw resources away from the Low Countries. In addition, the prolonged fighting toughened the French armies and brought through a number of talented generals, the chief amongst whom were Henri de la Tour d'Auvergne, Vicomte de Turenne, and Louis II Bourbon, Prince de Condé. It was Condé, then Duc d'Enghien (he became Prince de Condé on his father's death in 1646), who beat the veteran Spanish Army of Flanders at Rocroi in 1643. This victory, whilst over-rated in French mythology, was a significant moment in the

French officer

development of the French army, and probably marks the beginning of the ascendancy of France over Spain on the battlefield.

By the mid-1640s French armies were starting to campaign in Germany on a regular basis. Firstly that of Turenne, who had taken command of the Armee d'Allemagne, based around the Bernhardine troops which had transferred to French service on the death of Sachsen-Weimar, and then also armies under Condé. These beat the Imperialists in the battles of Freiburg in 1644 and Allerheim (also known as the second Battle of Nördlingen) in 1645, although both were bloody affairs, with the French losing huge numbers of casualties. Condé, especially, was very cavalier with the lives of his troops, although he always shared their dangers, leading from the front. Turenne was more sparing with their lives, but often had to serve under Condé who, being a Prince of the blood, outranked him.

In 1642 Richelieu, the architect of France's policy for the war, died and was followed in 1643, five days before the battle of Rocroi, by Louis XIII. The new king, his son Louis XIV, was a minor aged five. His mother, Anne of Austria, became regent. Control of policy was effectively in the hands of Richelieu's successor, the Italian Cardinal Mazarin. Despite the change of regime, there was no change in French policy.

In 1648 the Peace of Westphalia brought the Thirty Years' War to a close. However, it did not include the French war with Spain, which was to continue for another decade. Also, just as the Peace of Westphalia was being signed, a series of civil wars known as the Frondes broke out in France.

This list covers French armies from the entry of the French into the mainstream of the Thirty Years' War in 1635 until the Peace of Westphalia and the outbreak of the Frondes in 1648.

TROOP NOTES

The pike of the Guard infantry regiments and the established Vieux and Petits Vieux regiments in theory remained armoured in this period, but, as with most other armies, the practicalities of campaigning meant that this was often discarded. It is very unlikely that many, if any, of the new infantry regiments raised in this period were issued with significant amounts of armour; some did not have pikes in the later stages of the war.

During this period French infantry continued to utilise a rapid advance to close combat as described under the Early 17th Century French list. We represent this by limiting French infantry to Musket* capability but give them Impact Foot capability in addition. Despite this aggressive tendency, on occasion field fortifications were used.

Whilst numbers of guards and Vieux troops were high, as they were larger than usual regiments, they were not concentrated but rather a small number of battalions from them were posted to separate armies.

French armies fighting in Catalonia contained a high proportion of militia units as the better units were deployed to the armies fighting in northern France and Germany.

In the early stages of their participation in the war, French armies contained a relatively low proportion of cavalry, and these continued to fight in deeper formations than most contemporary cavalry according to Montecuccoli writing in about 1640. By the time of Rocroi in 1643, however, cavalry numbers had significantly increased and they appear to have fought in a similar manner to most other cavalry of the time.

Under Swedish influence many infantry regiments had small 4-pounder cannon attached to them. However, around 1643 these were taken away and concentrated with the other artillery.

Guard pikeman

THIRTY YEARS' WAR FRENCH STARTER ARMY		
Commander-in-Chief	1	Field Commander
Sub-Commanders	2	2 x Troop Commander
Chevaux-légers, Gendarmerie or Carabins	1 BG	4 bases of chevaux-légers, gendarmerie or carabins: Superior, Armoured, Determined Horse – Impact Pistol, Melee Pistol
Chevaux-légers, Gendarmerie or Carabins	1 BG	4 bases of chevaux-légers, gendarmerie or carabins: Average, Armoured, Determined Horse– Impact Pistol, Melee Pistol
Chevaux-légers, Gendarmerie or Carabins	2 BGs	Each comprising 4 bases of chevaux-légers, gendarmerie or carabins: Average, Unarmoured, Horse – Impact Pistol, Melee Pistol
Forlorn Hope Carabins	1 BG	4 bases of forlorn hope carabins: Average, Unarmoured, Light Horse – Carbine, Melee Pistol
Guard and Vieux infantry	1 BG	6 bases of guard and vieux infantry: 2 Superior, Unarmoured, Heavy Foot – Pike; and 4 Superior, Unarmoured, Medium Foot – Musket*, Impact Foot
Petits Vieux and new infantry	2 BGs	Each comprising 6 bases of petits vieux and new infantry: 2 Average, Unarmoured, Heavy Foot – Pike; and 4 Average, Unarmoured, Medium Foot – Musket*, Impact Foot
Petits Vieux and new infantry	1 BG	6 bases of petits vieux and new infantry: Average, Unarmoured, Medium Foot – Musket*, Impact Foot
Artillery	1 BG	2 bases of artillery: Average Heavy Artillery – Heavy Artillery
Camp	1	Unfortified camp
Total	10 BGs	Camp, 20 mounted bases, 26 foot bases, 3 commanders

BUILDING A CUSTOMISED LIST USING OUR ARMY POINTS

Choose an army based on the maxima and minima in the list below. The following special instructions apply to this army:

- Commanders should be depicted as Chevaux-légers.
- If any regimental guns are used at least as many Superior battle groups must have them as Average battle groups.
- Battle groups without pike are not allowed regimental guns.
- Superior quality infantry, Horse or Determined Horse cannot be used with Catalan War special campaigns options.
- Catalan tercios do not count as tercios as defined in the rule book.

THIRTY YEARS' WAR FRENCH

Territory Types: Agricultural, Woodland, Hilly

C-in-C	Great Commander/Field Commander/Troop Commander						80/50/35	1	
Sub-commanders	Field Commander						50	0–2	
	Troop Commander						35	0–3	

Troop name		Troop Type			Capabilities			Points per base	Bases per BG	Total bases
		Type	Armour	Quality	Shooting	Impact	Melee			
Core Troops										
Chevaux-légers, Gendarmerie or Carabins	Only before 1643	Horse	Armoured	Average	–	Pistol	Pistol	10	4	4–20
			Unarmoured					8		
		Horse	Armoured	Average	Carbine	–	Pistol	11	4	
			Unarmoured					9		
	Only from 1643	Determined Horse	Armoured	Superior	–	Pistol	Pistol	21	4	8–32
			Unarmoured					18		
		Determined Horse	Armoured	Average	–	Pistol	Pistol	15	4	
			Unarmoured					12		
		Horse	Armoured	Average	–	Pistol	Pistol	10	4	
			Unarmoured					8		
Forlorn hope Carabins		Light Horse	Unarmoured	Average	Carbine	–	Pistol	9	4	0–4
		Dragoons	Unarmoured	Average	Arquebus	–	–	7	4	
Guard and Vieux infantry		Medium Foot	Unarmoured	Superior	Musket*	Impact Foot	–	11	4	6	0–12
		Heavy Foot	Armoured	Superior	–	Pike	Pike	9	2	
		Medium Foot	Unarmoured	Superior	Musket*	Impact Foot	–	11	4	6
		Heavy Foot	Unarmoured	Superior	–	Pike	Pike	8	2	
Petits Vieux and new infantry	Any	Medium Foot	Unarmoured	Average	Musket*	Impact Foot	–	8	4	6	12–48	12–60
		Heavy Foot	Unarmoured	Average	–	Pike	Pike	5	2	
	Only from 1643	Medium Foot	Unarmoured	Average	Musket*	Impact Foot	–	7	6	0–24
Artillery	Any	Heavy Artillery	–	Average	Heavy Artillery	–	–	25	2	2–4
		Medium Artillery	–	Average	Medium Artillery	–	–	20	2,3 or 4	
	Only from 1643	Light Artillery	–	Average	Light Artillery	–	–	12	2,3 or 4	

Optional Troops										
4-pounder guns attached to infantry	Only before 1643	Regimental Guns	–	Superior / Average	Regimental Guns	Regimental Guns	–	12 / 9	n/a	0–1 per Guard, Vieux and Petits Vieux BG
Newly raised French infantry and militia	Medium Foot	Unarmoured	Poor	Musket*	Impact Foot	–	6	4	6	0–36
	Heavy Foot	Unarmoured	Poor	–	Pike	Pike	3	2		
Foreign infantry regiments	Medium Foot	Unarmoured	Average	Musket	–	–	8	4	6	0–24
	Heavy foot	Unarmoured	Average	–	Pike	Pike	5	2		
Dragoons	Dragoons	Unarmoured	Average	Musket	–	–	8	2,3 or 4		0–4
Ditches and barricades	Field Fortifications	–	–	–	–	–	3	–		0–20
Warships	Naval Units	–	Average	Naval	–	–	30	–		0–1

Allies
German allies – Later Thirty Years' War Germans (Protestant)
Weimarian allies (only before 1644) – Later Thirty Years' War Swedish and Weimarian
Swedish allies – Later Thirty Years' War Swedish and Weimarian
Dutch allies (only before 1640) – Later Eighty Years' War Dutch

Special Campaigns										
Catalan War from 1641 – no allies allowed										
French militia	Medium Foot	Unarmoured	Poor	Musket*	Impact Foot	–	6	4	6	24–48
	Heavy Foot	Unarmoured	Poor	–	Pike	Pike	3	2		
Catalan tercios and militia	Medium Foot	Unarmoured	Average	Musket	–	–	8	4	6	0–18
	Heavy Foot	Unarmoured	Average	–	Pike	Pike	5	2		
	Medium Foot	Unarmoured	Poor	Musket	–	–	6	4	6	
	Heavy Foot	Unarmoured	Poor	–	Pike	Pike	3	2		
Miquelets	Light Foot	Unarmoured	Average	Musket	–	–	7		6	6–18

THIRTY YEARS' WAR PENINSULAR SPANISH

*T*his list covers Spanish armies in the Iberian Peninsula from the beginning of the war with France in 1635 until the Treaty of the Pyrenees in 1659 freed the army to concentrate on its war with the rebellious Portuguese.

The military pressure on the French–Catalan border, combined with the aggressive fiscal and political measures of the Union de Armas of the Conde Duque de Olivares (Spain's prime minister) and a series of bad harvests, caused a revolution in Catalonia in 1640. Since Catalonia could not withstand Spanish power, the original idea of an independent Republic was abandoned, and the Crown offered to Louis XIII of France. Despite the fact that French efforts were hampered by the effects of their internal conflicts (Fronde), and that Catalonia officially abandoned the war after the siege of Barcelona in 1652, the war lasted until the signing of the Treaty of the Pyrenees in 1659.

Parallel to the Catalan revolt, Portugal also rebelled in 1640, claiming its independence. This third front (after the Low Countries and the Pyrenees) was just too much for Spanish resources and they were never able to send enough troops to break Portuguese resistance. After an initial Spanish success at Montijo in 1644, the Portuguese defeated the Spanish army at Elvas in 1659, Estremoz in 1663 and finally at Villaviciosa in 1665. Spain recognised Portuguese independence with the Treaty of Lisbon in 1668.

TROOP NOTES

Some old Tercios and foreign regiments were moved to the Peninsula in order to reinforce the French border, but newly raised Tercios were also needed to sustain this second battlefront. The new units were originally called "Temporary" or "Auxiliary" tercios and were to be 1,000 men strong and proved to be of variable quality. From 1637 "Provincial tercios" were created, theoretically 1,200 men strong, and were a more selective levy leading to better quality units.

As with the tercios in other Spanish armies, the actual strengths in the

Arquebusier

field were somewhat below their paper strength, although up until c.1640 strengths of 1,000 men or more were still common. By around 1643, however, this had fallen to closer to 600 men. We classify the larger formations as Later Tercios.

In respect of their weaponry, the tercios raised in the Iberian peninsular initially still had more arquebusiers than musketeers in their shot, but their equipment progressively improved until it matched the standards of other contemporary armies, being mostly musket armed.

Miquelets were irregular troops armed with matchlock muskets and pistols, capable of either sniping or delivering heavy fire from ambushes before retiring under cover. They emerged to fight against the Spanish army during the Catalan revolt, but after the surrender of the Catalan Government in 1652, a sort of civil war started in Catalonia between those still supporting the French party, and those that preferred to come back to Spanish rule. From that moment Miquelet parties were also raised by the Spanish in order to fight the regular French army as well as the Miquelets still fighting for France.

Officer

THIRTY YEARS' WAR PENINSULAR SPANISH STARTER ARMY

Commander-in-Chief	1	Field Commander
Sub-Commanders	2	2 x Troop Commander
Guardias Viejas	1 BG	4 bases of guardias viejas: Superior, Armoured, Cavaliers – Light Lancers, Swordsmen
Caballos corazas	2 BGs	Each comprising 4 bases of caballos corazas: Average, Armoured, Horse – Impact Pistol, Melee Pistol
Arquebusiers	1 BG	4 bases of arquebusiers: Average, Armoured, Horse – Carbine, Melee Pistol
Provincial Tercios	3 BGs	Each comprising 6 bases of provincial tercios: 2 Average, Armoured, Heavy Foot – Pike; and 4 Average, Unarmoured, Medium Foot – Musket
Foreign regiments not in tercio formation	1 BG	6 bases of foreign regiments not in tercio formation: 2 Average, Unarmoured, Heavy Foot, Pike; and 4 Average, Unarmoured, Medium Foot - Musket
Miquelets	1 BG	6 bases of miquelets: Average, Unarmoured, Light Foot – Musket
Dragoons	1 BG	3 bases of dragoons: Average, Unarmoured, Dragoons – Musket
Field guns	1 BG	2 bases of field guns: Average Medium Artillery – Medium Artillery
Camp	1	Unfortified camp
Total	11 BGs	Camp, 16 mounted bases, 33 foot bases, 3 commanders

BUILDING A CUSTOMISED LIST USING OUR ARMY POINTS

Choose an army based on the maxima and minima in the list below. The following special instructions apply to this army:

- Commanders should be depicted as Guardias Viejas.
- Battle groups designated "(LT)" count as later tercios as defined in the rule book.

THIRTY YEARS' WAR PENINSULAR SPANISH

Territory Types: Agricultural, Hilly

Troop name		Troop Type			Capabilities			Points per base	Bases per BG	Total bases
C-in-C		Great Commander/Field Commander/Troop Commander						80/50/35	1	
Sub-commanders		Field Commander						50	0–2	
		Troop Commander						35	0–3	
		Type	Armour	Quality	Shooting	Combat	Melee			
Core Troops										
Guardias viejas		Cavaliers	Armoured	Superior	–	Pistol	Pistol	19	2–4	0–4
		Cavaliers	Armoured	Superior	–	Light Lancers	Swordsmen	19	2–4	
Caballos corazas	Only from 1640	Determined Horse	Armoured	Superior	–	Pistol	Pistol	21	4	0–8
	Any	Horse	Heavily Armoured	Superior	–	Pistol	Pistol	16	4	
		Horse	Heavily Armoured	Average	–	Pistol	Pistol	12	4	4–12
		Horse	Armoured	Average	–	Pistol	Pistol	10	4	

SCOTS COVENANTER

Troop name	Date	Troop type	Armour	Quality	Shooting	Impact	Melee	Points	Bases	Per BG	Total
Arquebusiers		Horse	Armoured	Average	Carbine	–	Pistol	11		4	4–8
			Unarmoured					9			
Old tercio foot	Only before 1643	Medium Foot	Unarmoured	Superior	Musket	–	–	11	6	9 (LT)	0–18
		Heavy Foot	Armoured	Superior	–	Pike	Pike	9	3		
		Medium Foot	Unarmoured	Average	Musket	–	–	8	6	9 (LT)	
		Heavy foot	Armoured	Average	–	Pike	Pike	6	3		
	Only from 1644	Medium Foot	Unarmoured	Superior	Musket	–	–	11	4	6	
		Heavy Foot	Armoured	Superior	–	Pike	Pike	9	2		
		Medium Foot	Unarmoured	Average	Musket	–	–	8	4	6	
		Heavy Foot	Armoured	Average	–	Pike	Pike	6	2		
"Temporary" or "Auxiliary" tercios	Only before 1637	Medium Foot	Unarmoured	Poor	Arquebus	–	–	5	6	9 (LT)	18–72
		Heavy Foot	Armoured	Poor	–	Pike	Pike	3	3		
Provincial Tercios	Only from 1637 to 1643	Medium Foot	Unarmoured	Average	Arquebus	–	–	7	6	9 (LT)	18–72
		Heavy Foot	Armoured	Average	–	Pike	Pike	6	3		
	Only from 1644	Medium Foot	Unarmoured	Average	Musket	–	–	8	4	6	
		Heavy Foot	Armoured		–	Pike	Pike	6	2		
Field guns		Medium Artillery	–	Average	Medium Artillery	–	–	20	2, 3 or 4		2–4
Heavy guns		Heavy Artillery	–	Average	Heavy Artillery	–	–	25	2		
Optional Troops											
Newly raised tercios	Only from 1637 to 1643	Medium Foot	Unarmoured	Poor	Arquebus	–	–	5	6	9 (LT)	0–30
		Heavy Foot	Armoured	Poor	–	Pike	Pike	4	3		
	Only from 1644	Medium Foot	Unarmoured	Poor	Musket	–	–	6	4	6	
		Heavy Foot	Armoured	Poor	–	Pike	Pike	4	2		
Foreign regiments not in tercio formation	Only before 1644	Medium Foot	Unarmoured	Average	Musket	–	–	8	4	6	0–18
		Heavy Foot	Armoured		–	Pike	Pike	6	2		
	Only from 1644	Medium Foot	Unarmoured	Average	Musket	–	–	8	4	6	
		Heavy Foot	Unarmoured		–	Pike	Pike	5	2		
Dragoons		Dragoons	Unarmoured	Average	Musket	–	–	8	3 or 4		0–6
Warships		Naval Units	–	Average	Naval	–	–	30	–		0–1
Miquelets	Only after 1652	Light Foot	Unarmoured	Average	Musket	–	–	7	6–8		6–18

SCOTS COVENANTER

Scotland of the mid-17th century was defined by religion. In the highlands Catholicism prevailed, but for the vast majority in the lowlands it was the Presbyterian church of John Knox which dominated. Their religion was free from ceremony, and the ministers so dour that even the English Puritans would have been regarded as too fun loving and fond of frippery.

The Scottish kirk had existed uneasily alongside the Church of England despite failed efforts to create a closer union of religious practice. King James had known when to leave things alone, but his son Charles I decided to impose the English prayer book on Scotland.

The first reading from the prayer book in Edinburgh ended in a riot with the unfortunate dean being assaulted, a situation that was repeated throughout the land – other than in Brechin, where the preacher laid a brace of pistols alongside the prayer book on the pulpit to retain his congregation's peaceful attention. The next act was rebellious in its nature, when two leading churchmen composed the "Solemn League and Covenant" which would become a contract between the Scots and God,

Infantry of the Solemn League and Covenant, 1644, by Angus McBride © Osprey Publishing Ltd. Taken from Elite 25: Soldiers of the English Civil War (1): Infantry.

making the Scots the new chosen people. The first Covenant was signed by the nobles, led by James Graham, Earl (and later Marquis) of Montrose, and Archibald Campbell, Earl of Argyll. This was followed by the production of thousands more copies, which were signed by the common folk, frequently in blood.

Charles at first attempted to reach a peaceful solution, but was eventually forced to resort to arms, leading to the Bishops' Wars. Both were a total failure for Charles, who was forced to make a humiliating truce with the Covenanters, and pay them substantial expenses for the privilege of the Scots occupying Northern England.

Other than sending regiments to Ireland to protect Scots settlers, Scotland remained aloof from the growing troubles in England and Ireland, but was being courted by both Royalists and Parliamentarians. Eventually the Scots agreed to join the Parliamentarians, not so much for the financial inducements offered, but on the understanding that England would sign the Covenant and the English church follow Scotland's practices. The Scots army was sent into England, where it formed the major part of the allied army which defeated Rupert at Marston Moor. Other than minor actions and sieges, however, the army fought no other major engagement, mainly because trouble was brewing at home.

Montrose, a signatory of the Covenant, but now a born-again Royalist, had been sent into Scotland by Charles to raise a Royalist army and fight the Covenanters in their own backyard. His victories over the next year brought the Covenanters to the edge of disaster, and led to the recall of many of the best regiments from England. Finally, the remnants of Montrose's army was crushed by a mainly mounted Covenanting army at Philiphaugh.

In 1646, with the war lost, King Charles surrendered himself at Newark to the Scots, who tried to persuade him to sign the Covenant and accept the primacy of the Presbyterian church in all his three kingdoms. This was too much even for Charles, who refused. Frustrated, the Scots handed him over to Parliament in exchange for £200,000. This was a bad move, as with the King in their hands the Parliamentarians no longer had any reason to make concessions to the Scots, nor indeed sign the Covenant.

As a result of this disappointment, the Covenanters split into several factions. One of these factions, the "Engagers", supported the King and joined the English Royalists. They were defeated at the battle of Preston by Cromwell, who then marched into Scotland, and with Argyll's help, crushed opposition there.

A period of peace seemed likely, but this ended with the execution of Charles the First by the English parliament in 1649. Within five days the Covenanters declared his son, Charles II, King of the three Kingdoms. Charles arrived in Scotland to accept his legacy, but was only to be allowed ashore if he signed the Covenant and accepted the reduced view of his kingship. Charles accepted, but would bide his time for revenge, not only for this humiliation but for the fact that it was the Covenanters who had handed his father over to Cromwell in the first place. More immediate

Covenanters engage Royalist foot

problems for the Scots lay ahead, as Cromwell descended on Scotland, defeated the Scots at Dunbar and then pursued them to Worcester for a final reckoning.

This list covers Scottish armies of the Covenant from the First Bishop's war in 1639 to Cromwell's conquest of Scotland in 1652. It also includes the forces sent to Ireland to intervene on behalf of Protestant Scottish settlers from 1642 until their final withdrawal in 1650.

TROOP NOTES

The Covenanting infantry, with a minister attached to each regiment for inspiration, were on the whole good steady foot, although local levies raised in Scotland were often of lower quality. Armour was also in short supply and most infantry could not even claim ownership of a buff coat, with these mostly being given to the cavalry. Before 1650 many regiments also struggled to reach the ratio of 2:1 of musket to pike, but the army that went into England in 1644 was much better equipped. The early Covenanting armies of the Bishops' Wars period were even worse, with many troops equipped with an arquebus (or hagbutt or hagbut as it was known in Scotland).

These units also had a higher proportion of pike. Despite this deficiency, these troops are still classified as Musket*. The army in Ireland was also habitually short of muskets, with priority being given to the home army.

Allowance for Campbell of Lawers' regiment to be rated superior represents this unit's sterling performance at both Auldearn and Dunbar, where in both instances it was virtually annihilated after holding off superior enemy forces.

Campbell of Lawers' attack on Auldearn village, 1645, by Gerry Embleton © Osprey Publishing Ltd. Taken from Campaign 123: Auldearn 1645.

SCOTS COVENANTER

Scottish cavalry of this time initially favoured shooting at range with large bore pistols, some cavalrymen having as many as four of these and maybe a carbine as well, but as they were poorly mounted on native "light but weak nags" cannot be rated better than Poor. A re-adoption of the lance made some improvements to performance, with at first half then the whole of nearly all units being so armed – however, David Leslie's own regiment appears to have remained wholly firearm equipped. Despite this change they were still usually outclassed by most opposing horse, but their performance during the Preston campaign in 1648 and the Dunbar campaign of 1650 justifies them being Average quality rather than Poor; we assume this would apply earlier as well.

Dragoons were never common in Scottish armies, although during the Bishops' Wars there were "two or three thousand carraidge horses with swords and hagbutts". A downside of these improvised dragoons was that in 1639 the army was short of baggage animals and thus unable to invade England! The army of 1643/44 included a regiment of dragoons, but these converted into (poor) cavalry and after this only occasional dragoon troops are recorded.

Unregimented Highlander battle groups are graded as Musket* if they have a high proportion of men armed with musket or arquebus, Bow* if these are outnumbered by men armed with bow.

The army in Ireland could from time to time, depending on the political situation, call upon "British" cavalry of the Anglo–Irish garrisons who were of passable quality. On occasion infantry were also available in reasonable numbers, but such joint operations were not well co-ordinated and are best represented by the inclusion of an allied contingent.

Frame gun deployed for action

SCOTS COVENANTER STARTER ARMY (SCOTLAND 1645)			
Commander-in-Chief	1	Field Commander	
Sub-Commanders	2	2 x Troop Commander	
Horse	3 BG	Each comprising 4 bases of horse: Average, Unarmoured, Horse – Light Lancers, Swordsmen	
Campbell of Lawers' regiment	1 BG	6 bases of Campbell of Lawers' regiment: 2 Superior, Unarmoured, Heavy Foot – Pike; and 4 Superior, Unarmoured, Medium Foot – Musket	
Foot Regiments	3 BGs	Each comprising 6 bases of foot regiments: 2 Average, Unarmoured, Heavy Foot – Pike; and 4 Average, Unarmoured, Medium Foot – Musket	
Foot Regiments	3 BGs	Each comprising 6 bases of foot regiments: 2 Poor, Unarmoured, Heavy Foot – Pike; and 4 Poor, Unarmoured, Medium Foot – Musket*	
Unregimented Highlanders	1 BG	8 bases of unregimented highlanders: 8 Average, Unarmoured, Warriors – Musket*, Impact Foot, Swordsmen,	
Dragoons	1 BG	2 bases of dragoons: Average, Unarmoured, Dragoons – Musket	
Frames or similar light artillery	1 BG	3 bases of frames: Average, Light Artillery - Light Artillery	
Camp	1	Unfortified camp	
Total	13 BGs	Camp, 12 mounted bases, 55 foot bases, 3 commanders	

BUILDING A CUSTOMISED LIST USING OUR ARMY POINTS

Choose an army based on the maxima and minima in the list below. The following special instructions apply to this army:

- Commanders should be depicted as Horse.
- Scots armies in Ireland need not take otherwise compulsory Horse and cannot take more than the minimum if they do take any.

- Scots armies in Ireland cannot use Dragoons or Moss Troopers.
- Armies from 1642 to 1649 can only have one more non-Lancer Horse battle group than they have Lancer Horse battle groups.
- "Engager" armies in 1648 cannot use artillery.
- Minima marked * only apply if English Royalists are fielded in which case all the English form an allied contingent.

SCOTS COVENANTER									
Territory Types: Agricultural, Hilly, Woodland									
C-in-C		Great Commander/Field Commander/Troop Commander					80/50/35	1	
Sub-commanders		Field Commander					50	0–2	
		Troop Commander					35	0–3	
Troop name		Troop Type			Capabilities		Points per base	Bases per BG	Total bases
		Type	Armour	Quality	Shooting	Impact	Melee		
Core Troops									
Horse	Only before 1642	Horse	Unarmoured	Poor	Pistol	–	Pistol	7	4	4–24
	Only from 1642 to 1649	Horse	Unarmoured	Average	–	Light Lancers	Swordsmen	8	4	4–24
				Poor				6		
		Horse	Unarmoured	Poor	Pistol	–	Pistol	7	4	
	Only from 1650	Horse	Unarmoured	Average	Pistol	–	Pistol	9	4	0–4	4–24
		Horse	Unarmoured	Average	–	Light Lancers	Swordsmen	8	4	4–24	
				Poor				6			
Foot regiments	Only before 1642 or in Ireland	Medium Foot	Unarmoured	Average	Musket*	–	–	7	4	6	0–60	24–168
		Heavy Foot	Unarmoured	Average	–	Pike	Pike	5	2			
		Medium Foot	Unarmoured	Poor	Musket*	–	–	5	4	6	18–120	
		Heavy Foot	Unarmoured	Poor	–	Pike	Pike	3	2			
	Only from 1642 to 1649 except in England in 1644	Medium Foot	Unarmoured	Average	Musket	–	–	8	4	6	0–36	24–168
		Heavy Foot	Unarmoured	Average	–	Pike	Pike	5	2			
		Medium Foot	Unarmoured	Poor	Musket*	–	–	5	4	6	18–120	
		Heavy Foot	Unarmoured	Poor	–	Pike	Pike	3	2			
	Only from 1650 in Scotland and England	Medium Foot	Unarmoured	Average	Musket	–	–	8	4	6	18–96	24–120
		Heavy Foot	Unarmoured	Average	–	Pike	Pike	5	2			
		Medium Foot	Unarmoured	Poor	Musket	–	–	6	4	6	0–60	
		Heavy Foot	Unarmoured	Poor	–	Pike	Pike	3	2			
Heavy artillery		Heavy Artillery	–	Average	Heavy Artillery	–	–	25	2, 3 or 4	0–4
Medium artillery		Medium Artillery	–	Average	Medium Artillery	–	–	20	2, 3 or 4	
Frames or similar light artillery	Only armies outside Ireland	Light Artillery	–	Average	Light Artillery	–	–	12	2, 3 or 4	2–8

Optional Troops											
Campbell of Lawers regiment	Only in Scotland 1645 to 1650	Medium Foot	Unarmoured	Superior	Musket	–	–	11	4	6	0–6
		Heavy Foot	Unarmoured	Superior	–	Pike	Pike	8	2		
Unregimented highlanders	Only in Scotland 1644 to 1645	Warriors	Unarmoured	Average / Poor	Bow*	Impact Foot	Swordsmen	7 / 5	6–8		0–12
		Warriors	Unarmoured	Average / Poor	Musket*	Impact Foot	Swordsmen	8 / 6	6–8		
Dragoons	Only before 1642	Dragoons	Unarmoured	Average	Arquebus	–	–	7	3 or 4		0–9
	Only from 1642 to 1644	Dragoons	Unarmoured	Average	Musket	–	–	8	2, 3 or 4		0–4
	Only from 1645	Dragoons	Unarmoured	Average	Musket	–	–	8	2		0–2
Moss troopers	Only from 1650	Light Horse	Unarmoured	Average	Pistols	Light Lancers	Swordsmen	10	4		0–4

Allies											
Only in Ireland 1642 – 1650											
"British" allies – Early Caroline English											

Special Campaigns											
Only in Ireland 1642 – 1650 (no allies allowed)											
"British" cavalry		Horse	Unarmoured	Average	Pistols	–	Pistols	9	4		0–8

Only in England in 1644

Optionally up to half the army's points can be spent on troops from the English Civil War Parliamentarian army list. If so, Foot and Horse minima from that list must be adhered to, but otherwise any troops may be selected. All generals count as in line of command to all troops in the army regardless of nationality. This represents the allied army at the siege of York and the Battle of Marston Moor.

	Type	Armour	Quality				Pts			
Foot	Medium Foot	Unarmoured	Average	Musket	–	–	8	4	6	12–72
	Heavy Foot	Unarmoured	Average	–	Pike	Pike	5	2		
	Medium Foot	Unarmoured	Poor	Musket*	–	–	5	4	6	12–24
	Heavy Foot	Unarmoured	Poor	–	Pike	Pike	3	2		

Only in Scotland in 1645 – Battle of Philiphaugh

All cavalry minima and maxima are tripled and all are Average quality. All dragoons minima and maxima are tripled. Only one infantry regiment can be fielded and that must be Average quality. No highlanders can be fielded. No artillery can be fielded.

Only "Engagers" in England in 1648

English Allied commander (Sir Marmaduke Langdale)	Field Commander/Troop Commander						40/25		*1	
English Royalist horse	Cavaliers	Unarmoured	Average	–	Pistol	Pistol	11	4	*4	
English Royalist infantry	Medium Foot	Unarmoured	Average	Musket	–	–	8	4	6	*6–18	*12–24
	Heavy Foot	Unarmoured	Average	–	Pike	Pike	5	2		
	Medium Foot	Unarmoured	Poor	Musket	–	–	6	4	6	0–12
	Heavy Foot	Unarmoured	Poor	–	Pike	Pike	3	2		

SCOTS ROYALIST

This list covers the Scottish Armies that supported King Charles against the forces of the Covenant in Scotland. The first army was raised in 1639 by the Marquis of Huntly to oppose the Covenanters led by Montrose, but this venture was short-lived, with the army being disbanded shortly thereafter.

The Royalist army which receives most historical attention was that which operated under the Marquis of Montrose, who had changed sides in the interim period, during the years 1644 to 1645. From arriving in Scotland as a one man army after Marston Moor, Montrose quickly raised a mixed bag of Irish professional soldiers, highlanders and pike and shot armed foot. This army won a string of victories against Covenanting opposition of varying quality, but was finally crushed at Philiphaugh in September 1645 when confronted by a vastly superior mounted Covenanting force.

Montrose did raise the king's standard again in April 1650, but his rag tag army was crushed quickly at Carbisdale. He himself was dragged off to Edinburgh to be executed and, thereafter, while no doubt a talented general, achieved a somewhat undeserved legendary status in Scottish history of being a military genius. Interestingly it was his deputy McColla, who history generally regards as no more than a hot blooded Irishman who Montrose often had to rescue, who may in fact have been the real professional soldier in the army.

The cavalry battle at Alford, 1645, by Gerry Embleton © Osprey Publishing Ltd. Taken from Campaign 123: Auldearn 1645.

TROOP NOTES

The Royalist Army which served under Montrose in 1644 and 1645 was inaccurately promoted by historians for many years as achieving their great victories solely as a result of wild highland charges, which swept away the opposition who were terrified by the fanatical assault. In practice, the composition of the army, and the armament with which it was equipped, changed continually during the period, with the numbers of highlanders, Irish, cavalry and pike and shot armed foot varying from battle to battle. The highlanders, in particular, tended to disappear as soon as they had gathered sufficient loot to take home and impress their relatives. They were, therefore, not troops to be relied upon in a long campaign, with the Irish Brigade, the pike and shot foot and latterly the cavalry being the mainstay of the army. Interestingly, the largest turn out of highlanders was at the battle of Inverlochy, where the clansmen seemed more interested in giving their traditional foes the Campbells a bloody nose than in supporting the King. True to form they disappeared back to their homes shortly thereafter.

To be fair to Montrose, he was one of those few individuals who genuinely seemed to be able to empathise with highlanders, gain their respect, and bring the best out of them. This was demonstrated best at Inverlochy, where highlanders were on both sides. Montrose fought dismounted with his highlanders, while his opponent Argyll watched the battle from a galley in the middle of the loch, and sailed away when he perceived that things were not going well.

Dragoons

The reasons for Montrose's victories in fact tended to vary depending on the circumstances. In 1644, when the opposition was mainly Covenanting levies, the discipline of the Irish Brigade was the principle difference, while in 1645 an increasing strong cavalry arm can be seen as a vital part of the victories.

Interestingly, the army raised by the Marquis of Huntly in 1639 was the best equipped Royalist army of the period in Scotland, as shipments of armour etc. from the King allowed Huntly to provide the Strathbogie Regiment with armour for its pikemen as well as raising a small cuirassier cavalry unit. The Strathbogie regiment also turned out with Montrose (without armour) and were highly regarded as one of the best units in the army – hence their superior rating. This is in strict contrast to Kilpont's regiment at Tippermuir, who fought on the Royalist side but actually thought they were being taken to fight for the Covenant. After the battle, when the regiment discovered that they had been misled, they murdered Kilpont and disappeared into the hills.

It should be noted that the armies in Scotland were invariably small and, therefore, troop scale is towards the low end, as without this armies could not be properly represented on the tabletop. The army lists that follow do place historical restriction on choice, but equally represent the changing balance of forces that served under Montrose and Huntly at different times. On most battlefields the composition of the army of Montrose will differ little from their Covenanting foes both in fighting style and armament.

Great care has been taken to rate this army in relation to the quality of the historical opposition, rather than endow it with the legendary and invincible status that earlier historians seemed determined to grant it. The only significant difference in troop capabilities is to allow the Irish Brigade to be rated as Swordsmen. This distinction is justified by the fact that Montrose in several key moments ordered them to set aside their pikes and muskets and close with their swords. In the recorded instances this was a highly successful tactic.

SCOTS ROYALIST STARTER ARMY (MONTROSE 1645)		
Commander-in-Chief	1	Field Commander
Sub-Commanders	2	2 x Troop Commander
Horse	2 BG	Each comprising 4 bases of horse: Average, Unarmoured, Horse – Shooting Pistol, Melee Pistol
Irish Brigade	2 BG	Each comprising 6 bases of Irish brigade: 2 Average, Unarmoured, Heavy Foot – Pike; and 4 Average, Unarmoured, Medium Foot – Musket, Swordsmen
Strathbogie Regiment	1 BG	6 bases of Strathbogie regiment: 2 Superior, Unarmoured, Heavy Foot – Pike; and 4 Superior, Unarmoured, Medium Foot – Musket
Scottish Foot	2 BGs	Each comprising 6 bases of Scottish foot: 2 Average, Unarmoured, Heavy Foot – Pike; and 4 Average, Unarmoured, Medium Foot – Musket
Scottish Foot	1 BG	6 bases of Scottish foot: 2 Poor, Unarmoured, Heavy Foot – Pike; and 4 Poor, Unarmoured, Medium Foot – Musket
McCollas' Bodyguard	1 BG	6 bases of McColla's bodyguard: 6 Superior, Unarmoured, Warriors – Bow*, Impact Foot, Swordsmen
Unregimented Highlanders	1 BG	8 bases of unregimented highlanders: 8 Average, Unarmoured, Warriors – Musket*, Impact Foot, Swordsmen
Dragoons	1 BG	2 bases of dragoons: Average, Unarmoured, Dragoons – Musket
Camp	1	Unfortified camp
Total	11 BGs	Camp, 8 mounted bases, 52 foot bases, 3 commanders

BUILDING A CUSTOMISED LIST USING OUR ARMY POINTS

Choose an army based on the maxima and minima in the list below. The following special instructions apply to this army:

- Commanders should be depicted as Horse or dismounted "Cavalier" style officers.

SCOTS ROYALIST

Territory Types: Hilly, Woodlands				
C-in-C	Great Commander/Field Commander/Troop Commander		80/50/35	1
Sub-commanders	Field Commander		50	0-2
	Troop Commander		35	0-3

Troop Name		Troop Type			Capabilities			Points per base	Bases Per BG		Total Bases
		Type	Armour	Quality	Shooting	Impact	Melee				
Core Troops											
Horse	Only in 1639	Horse	Unarmoured	Average	Pistol	–	Pistol	9	4		4-12
		Horse	Unarmoured	Poor	Pistol	–	Pistol	7	4		0-16
		Horse	Unarmoured	Average	–	Light Lancers	Swordsmen	8	4		0-4
		Horse	Unarmoured	Poor	–	Light Lancers	Swordsmen	6	4		4-20
	Only in 1645	Horse	Unarmoured	Average	Pistol	–	Pistol	9	4		4-12
		Horse	Unarmoured	Poor	Pistol	–	Pistol	7	4		0-8
		Horse	Unarmoured	Average	–	Light Lancers	Swordsmen	8	4		0-4
		Horse	Unarmoured	Poor	–	Light Lancers	Swordsmen	6	4		4-20
Scottish Foot	Only in 1639	Medium Foot	Unarmoured	Average	Musket	–	–	8	4	6	0-6
		Heavy Foot	Armoured	Average	–	Pike	Pike	6	2		
		Medium Foot	Unarmoured	Average	Musket	–	–	8	4	6	6-24
		Heavy Foot	Unarmoured	Average	–	Pike	Pike	5	2		
		Medium Foot	Unarmoured	Poor	Musket*	–	–	5	4	6	18-90
		Heavy Foot	Unarmoured	Poor	–	Pike	Pike	3	2		24-120
	Only in 1644	Medium Foot	Unarmoured	Average	Musket	–	–	8	4	6	0-12
		Heavy Foot	Unarmoured	Average	–	Pike	Pike	5	2		
		Medium Foot	Unarmoured	Poor	Musket	–	–	6	4	6	6-36
		Heavy Foot	Unarmoured	Poor	–	Pike	Pike	3	2		
		Medium Foot	Unarmoured	Poor	Musket*	–	–	5	4	6	6-42
		Heavy Foot	Unarmoured	Poor	–	Pike	Pike	3	2		12-90
	Only in 1645	Medium Foot	Unarmoured	Average	Musket	–	–	8	4	6	12-48
		Heavy Foot	Unarmoured	Average	–	Pike	Pike	5	2		
		Medium Foot	Unarmoured	Poor	Musket	–	–	6	4	6	6-36
		Heavy foot	Unarmoured	Poor	–	Pike	Pike	3	2		12-84
Irish Brigade	Only in 1644	Medium Foot	Unarmoured	Average	Musket	–	Swordsmen	9	4	6	12-24
		Heavy Foot	Unarmoured	Average	–	Pike	Pike	5	2		
	Only in 1645	Medium Foot	Unarmoured	Average	Musket	–	Swordsmen	9	4	6	6-18
		Heavy Foot	Unarmoured	Average	–	Pike	Pike	5	2		
Unregimented Highlanders	Warriors		Unarmoured	Average	Bow*	Impact Foot	Swordsmen	7	6-8		0-24
			Unarmoured	Average	Musket*	Impact Foot	Swordsmen	8	6-8		0-24 / 6-48
Optional Troops											
Cuirassiers	Only in 1639	Horse	Heavily Armoured	Poor	Pistol	–	Pistol	9	2		0-2
Moss Troopers	Only in 1644 and 1645	Light Horse	Unarmoured	Average	Pistol	Light Lancers	Swordsmen	10	4		0-4
Dragoons	Only in 1639 & 1645	Dragoons	Unarmoured	Average	Musket	–	–	8	2 or 3		0-3
McCollas' Bodyguard	Only in 1644 & 1645	Warriors	Unarmoured	Superior	Bow*	Impact Foot	Swordsmen	10	6		0-6
Strathbogie regiment	Only in 1645	Medium Foot	Unarmoured	Superior	Musket	–	–	11	4	6	0-6
		Heavy Foot	Unarmoured	Superior	–	Pike	Pike	8	2		
Frames or similar light artillery		Light Artillery	–	Poor	Light Artillery		—	9	2		0-2

The Irish Brigade, 1644–45, by Graham Turner © Osprey Publishing Ltd. Taken from Men-at-Arms 331: Scots Armies of the English Civil Wars.

EARLY RESTORATION PORTUGUESE

As a result of the financial burdens of the ongoing Spanish involvement in the Thirty Years' War, the Spanish government raised taxation levels on the Portuguese, despite Portugal being theoretically a separate state, although sharing the same king. Eventually this proved too much for the Portuguese and they rose in rebellion, proclaiming João, Duke of Braganza, their king as João IV.

Although Portugal was a small country compared to the Spanish empire, the Spanish, involved as they were with the war with France, were in no position to commit major forces to crush the rebellion. As a result the war proceeded in a rather desultory fashion, with only one real battle in this period, Montijo in 1644. Although this went badly for the Portuguese, with so few troops available the Spanish were unable to follow up their victory.

This list covers Portuguese armies from the beginning of the War of Restoration until the signature of the Treaty of the Pyrenees in 1659 allowed Spain to re-focus on defeating the Portuguese rebellion.

TROOP NOTES

The first Portuguese infantry units raised in 1640 followed the Spanish Tercio model. They first consisted of 10 Tercios, each with a theoretical strength of 2,000 men: 700 pike, 400 musketeers, 790 arquebusiers and 110 officers. Later the proportion of musketeers was increased, while the total size of each unit was downsized to a theoretical strength of around 1,500 men: 480 pike, 720 musketeers, 300 arquebusiers plus officers. However, in the only major pitched battle of the period (Montijo, 1644), the Portuguese

actually deployed regiments of around 600 men in standard pike and shot formations following the Dutch or French model, thus we do not give Portuguese battle groups tercio abilities.

Portuguese cavalry were also organised along the lines of their Spanish counterparts, but was considered to be inferior to that of their foes. Probably owing to that, Portuguese infantry regiments initially had quite a high proportion of pike in comparison to the Spanish (although not enough to justify a different representation), and made extensive use of chevaux-de-frise to deter the Spanish cavalry.

Foreign regiments represent the troops sent by other European powers to support the Portuguese front, such as the Dutch present at Montijo.

Portuguese forces were mostly based in castles and fortresses along the Spanish border, from where they conducted a skirmishing war based on raids against the Spanish positions.

Field guns in action

EARLY RESTORATION PORTUGUESE STARTER ARMY

Commander-in-Chief	1	Field Commander
Sub-Commanders	2	2 x Troop Commander
Cuirassiers	2 BGs	Each comprising 4 bases of cuirassiers: Average, Armoured, Horse – Impact Pistol, Melee Pistol
Arquebusiers	2 BGs	Each comprising 4 bases of arquebusiers: Average, Armoured, Horse – Carbine, Melee Pistol
Portuguese tercios	3 BGs	Each comprising 6 bases of Portuguese tercios: 2 Average, Armoured, Heavy Foot – Pike; and 4 Average, Unarmoured, Medium Foot – Musket
Foreign regiments	2 BGs	Each comprising 6 bases of foreign regiments: 2 Average, Unarmoured, Heavy Foot – Pike; and 4 Average, Unarmoured, Medium Foot – Musket
Dragoons	1 BG	4 bases of dragoons: Average, Unarmoured, Dragoons – Musket
Dragoons	1 BG	3 bases of dragoons: Average, Unarmoured, Dragoons – Musket
Field guns	1 BG	2 bases of field guns: Average Medium Artillery – Medium Artillery
Camp	1	Unfortified camp
Total	12 BGs	Camp, 16 mounted bases, 39 foot bases, 3 commanders

BUILDING A CUSTOMISED LIST USING OUR ARMY POINTS

Choose an army based on the maxima and minima in the list below. The following special instructions apply to this army:

- Commanders should be depicted as cuirassiers.
- Portuguese tercios do not count as tercios as defined in the rule book.

EARLY RESTORATION PORTUGUESE

Territory Types: Agricultural

C-in-C		Great Commander/Field Commander/Troop Commander						80/50/35		1	
Sub-commanders		Field Commander						50		0–2	
		Troop Commander						35		0–3	
Troop name		Troop Type			Capabilities			Points per base	Bases per BG	Total bases
		Type	Armour	Quality	Shooting	Combat	Melee			
Core Troops											
Cuirassiers		Horse	Heavily Armoured	Average	–	Pistol	Pistol	12	4	0–12
		Horse	Armoured	Average	–	Pistol	Pistol	10	4	
Arquebusiers		Horse	Armoured	Average	Carbine	–	Pistol	11	4	4–8
			Unarmoured					9		
Portuguese tercios	Only before 1645	Medium foot	Unarmoured	Average	Arquebus	–	–	7	4	6	18–72
		Heavy Foot	Armoured	Average	–	Pike	Pike	6	2	
	Only from 1645	Medium foot	Unarmoured	Average	Musket	–	–	8	4	6
		Heavy foot	Armoured	Average	–	Pike	Pike	6	2	
Field guns		Medium Artillery	–	Average	Medium Artillery	–	–	20	2, 3 or 4	2–4
Optional Troops											
Newly raised Portuguese tercios and militia	Only before 1645	Medium foot	Unarmoured	Poor	Arquebus	–	–	5	4	6	0–48
		Heavy foot	Armoured	Poor	–	pike	pike	4	2	
	Only from 1645	Medium foot	Unarmoured	Poor	Musket	–	–	6	4	6
		Heavy foot	Armoured	Poor	–	Pike	Pike	4	2	
Foreign regiments		Medium foot	Unarmoured	Average	Musket	–	–	8	4	6	0–18
		Heavy foot	Unarmoured	Average	–	Pike	Pike	5	2	
Dragoons		Dragoons	Unarmoured	Average	Musket	–	–	8	3 or 4	0–6
Chevaux-de-frise to cover half the bases of each Portuguese tercio		Portable Defences	–	–	–	–	–	3		Any

CONFEDERATE IRISH

Ireland was, as always, very much the odd one out of the three Stuart kingdoms ruled by Charles I. The most obvious difference was that the majority of the population were Catholic, but thanks to a long series of English laws, were second class citizens because of this. Additionally, those very same laws had been enacted to encourage English settlers to move to Ireland and effectively to dispossess the Catholic population. Thus, hopefully, Ireland would eventually be turned into a Protestant kingdom. To add extra spice to the mix there were, in Ulster, a significant number of Presbyterian Scottish settlers, who naturally looked to their homeland for protection in times of trouble.

By 1641 the various pressures on the Irish proved too much and a rebellion broke out. The Irish organised themselves under the Irish Catholic Confederation, also known as the Confederation of Kilkenny after the city where it was based. They organised the rebels into military districts which were responsible for providing a number of troops for a combined "marching army", and additional troops for "home defence" of each region. Inevitably, the rebellion forced an English reaction, with a new army being raised in England for service in Ireland, but it also forced a reaction in Scotland, where a force of 10,000 men was despatched by the Covenanter government to Ulster for the protection of the Scots settlers.

The initial stages of the resulting war saw little in the way of pitched battles, and what there were went against the Irish. The majority of the fighting was of the "small war" variety, where the traditional hit and run tactics of the Irish once again proved effective and dragged the conflict on and on.

By late 1643, with the civil war turning against him, Charles ordered the Duke of Ormonde, his commander in Ireland, to organise a cessation of hostilities and the shipping to England of as many troops as possible to fight in his armies. This was done, and the war entered a stalemate.

The Irish cause was reinvigorated in 1645 by the arrival of Giovanni Battista Rinuccini, the Papal nuncio, with arms and money to encourage Catholic resistance against the Protestant English and Scots. His backing of more militant Confederates, such as Owen Roe O'Neill, ensured the continuation of the war. However, this also coincided with the winding down of hostilities in England, which allowed the English Parliament to send reinforcements to the forces loyal to them in Ireland.

Finally, in 1649, the English Parliament dispatched a high quality force from the New Model army, led by Oliver Cromwell, to finish the Irish war. This he did efficiently, although also with some brutality as the massacres at Drogheda and Wexford show.

This list covers Irish armies of the Confederation of Kilkenny from the outbreak of the rebellion in 1641 until their final defeat by the English Commonwealth in 1652. It includes Ormond's coalition army of 1648–50, comprised of a bizarre alliance of Confederate Irish, Irish and English Royalists and Presbyterian Ulster Scots.

TROOP NOTES

Whilst Irish foot were supposed to be organised into conventional regiments, modern weapons were in short supply and many were equipped in a more traditional manner and fought as they had for centuries. Those regiments that were equipped properly still suffered from a shortage of firearms and so are classified as Musket* – in fact even this may be a touch generous.

Irish horse were few in number and relatively ineffective, even being afraid of the fairly weak Scottish cavalry – asking for armour before they would be willing to fight them on one occasion. However, the cavalry of the coalition army of Ormond appears to have been both more numerous and of higher quality, even being able to stand up to the veteran English Commonwealth horse for a short time on occasion.

CONFEDERATE IRISH STARTER ARMY		
Commander-in-Chief	1	Field Commander
Sub-Commanders	2	2 x Troop Commander
Irish Horse	1 BG	4 bases of Irish horse: Poor, Unarmoured, Horse – Shooting Pistol, Swordsmen
Irish Horse	2 BGs	Each comprising 4 bases of Irish horse: Average, Unarmoured, Determined Horse – Impact Pistol, Melee Pistol
Irish Foot	4 BGs	Each comprising 6 bases of Irish foot: 2 Average, Unarmoured, Heavy Foot – Pike; and 4 Average, Unarmoured, Medium Foot – Musket*
Irish Foot	1 BG	8 bases of Irish foot: Average, Unarmoured, Warriors – Light Spear
"Redshanks"	2 BGs	Each comprising 8 bases of "Redshanks": Average, Unarmoured, Warriors – Bow*, Impact Foot, Swordsmen
Skirmishing Shot	2 BGs	Each comprising 4 bases of skirmishing shot: Average, Unarmoured, Light Foot – Musket
Camp	1	Unfortified camp
Total	12 BGs	Camp, 12 mounted bases, 56 foot bases, 3 commanders

BUILDING A CUSTOMISED LIST USING OUR ARMY POINTS

Choose an army based on the maxima and minima in the list below. The following special instructions apply to this army:

- Commanders should be depicted as Irish Horse.

CONFEDERATE IRISH									
Territory Types: Agricultural, Hilly, Woodland									
C-in-C		Great Commander/Field Commander/Troop Commander					80/50/35		1
Sub-commanders		Field Commander					50		0–3
		Troop Commander					35		
Troop name		**Troop Type**			**Capabilities**		Points per base	Bases per BG	Total bases
		Type	Armour	Quality	Shooting	Impact	Melee		
Core Troops									
Irish Horse	Any date	Horse	Unarmoured	Poor	Pistols	–	Swordsmen	7	4	4–8
	Only from 1648 to 1650	Determined Horse	Unarmoured	Average	–	Pistols	Pistols	12	4	0–12
Irish Foot		Medium Foot	Unarmoured	Average	Musket*	–	–	7	4	6	18–72	18–120
		Heavy Foot	Unarmoured	Average	–	Pike	Pike	5	2			
		Warriors	Unarmoured	Average	–	Light Spear	–	4	6–8	0–90	
Skirmishing shot		Light Foot	Unarmoured	Average	Musket	–	–	7	4–6	0–8
Optional Troops									
Irish militia regiments		Medium Foot	Unarmoured	Poor	Musket*	–	–	5	4	6	0–24
		Heavy Foot	Unarmoured	Poor	–	Pike	Pike	3	2		
Dragoons		Dragoons	Unarmoured	Average	Musket	–	–	8	2	0–2
"Redshanks"		Warriors	Unarmoured	Average	Bow*	Impact Foot	Swordsmen	7	6–8	0–36
Kerns with traditional weapons		Light Foot	Unarmoured	Average	Javelins	–	–	4	6–8	0–48
Demi-cannon or culverins		Heavy Artillery	–	Average	Heavy Artillery	–	–	25	2	0–2

EARLY ENGLISH CIVIL WAR ROYALIST

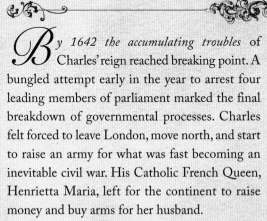

By 1642 the accumulating troubles of Charles' reign reached breaking point. A bungled attempt early in the year to arrest four leading members of parliament marked the final breakdown of governmental processes. Charles felt forced to leave London, move north, and start to raise an army for what was fast becoming an inevitable civil war. His Catholic French Queen, Henrietta Maria, left for the continent to raise money and buy arms for her husband.

Things started badly for Charles when the governor of Hull, Sir John Hotham, refused the King entry into the city, and thus prevented the stock of arms stored there since the Bishops' Wars

from being available to the King. With the navy also declaring for Parliament, Charles was desperately short of equipment and his armies were destined to be less well equipped than their enemies for much of the war.

Hostilities could be said to have formally started on 22 August 1642 when the King raised his standard in Nottingham. Recruits arrived only slowly and, faced by larger Parliamentarian forces under the Earl of Essex advancing from London, the King moved westwards where he could expect additional troops from loyal areas such as Wales. The manoeuvres in this area led to the first clash of any significance of the war, at Powick Bridge just outside Worcester. Here, although surprised, a force of Royalist cavalry led by the king's nephew, Prince Rupert, dramatically defeated a roughly equal sized force of Parliamentarian cavalry. This immediately gave the Royalist horse a morale advantage over the Parliamentarians, especially when Prince Rupert was present, that they were to retain for most of the war.

Battles of the English Civil War 1642–51 © Osprey Publishing Ltd. Taken from Essential Histories 58: The English Civil Wars 1642–1651.

EARLY ENGLISH CIVIL WAR ROYALIST

The first full field battle came shortly after Powick Bridge, at Edgehill. Here the Royalist cavalry again chased off most of their opposing numbers, however, in what was to become a feature of their behaviour throughout the war, they then left the field in uncontrolled pursuit of the routing Parliamentarians and headed for the enemy baggage. In the absence of the cavalry, the infantry of both sides then fought their own battle which, thanks to a handful of Parliamentarian cavalry that avoided the rout, went against the Royalists, although by the end of the day they had withdrawn in fair order, and the battle ended up as an indecisive draw. Under the influence of Prince Rupert, the Royalists then made a rapid advance on London via Reading. However, faced by the larger Parliamentarian army, bolstered by the London Trained Bands, at Turnham Green, they withdrew to Oxford for the winter. For the rest of the war Oxford was to be the King's capital.

In the following year, 1643, the war expanded to cover most of England. Initially things went well for the King, with victories in the north giving him control of most of Yorkshire, while in the south west the Cornish, led by Sir Ralph Hopton, embarked on a remarkable series of victories, often against superior numbers. Despite this, the King's armies remained short of firearms and, more importantly, short of powder, which led to their being unable to prosecute the war as strongly they would like and at times being forced to withdraw from Parliamentarian forces they might have been able to defeat.

The situation was improved in the summer of 1643 when, following the defeat and elimination of Sir William Waller's army at the Battle of Roundway Down (known to the Royalists as "Runaway Down"), the King's western forces were able to storm Bristol, the second city of the kingdom and location of a major armaments industry and, importantly, a port. However, despite this significant gain, the King was unable to capture Gloucester, a move which would have opened the road from Bristol to Oxford, and his army failed to defeat the Earl of Essex at the First Battle of Newbury (20 September) despite having placed itself between the Earl and his London base. Perhaps more significantly for the longer term, the army of the Parliamentarian Eastern Association, and their cavalry under Oliver Cromwell in particular, had won some victories in eastern counties.

This list covers English Civil War Royalist armies from the outbreak of the First Civil War until the effects of the Royalist capture of Bristol, and its associated arms industry, on 26th July 1643, were felt. During this period Royalist armies were often short of firearms and gunpowder compared to their Parliamentarian opponents. However, with Bristol producing 300 muskets per week, this was redressed, at least for the main Royalist armies. Those forces which benefitted from improved supplies are covered in the Later English Civil War Royalist list, whilst less well equipped armies are covered by this list until the end of the war.

Prince Rupert of the Rhine

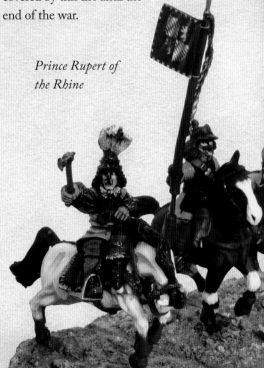

Royalist infantry, 1642, by Graham Turner © Osprey Publishing Ltd. Taken from Campaign 82: Edgehill 1642.

TROOP NOTES

At Edgehill in 1642 Prince Rupert attempted to have the infantry formed up in the Swedish fashion. Whether this meant the old Swedish brigade formation that the Swedes themselves had abandoned or something else is open to question. However, it is most unlikely that the recently levied infantry could have effectively used the Swedish brigade formation so it is not allowed even as an option.

At the start of the war Royalist dragoons were often armed with carbines rather than muskets and so are classified as having Arquebus capability.

The Cornish infantry were highly motivated, if somewhat ill-disciplined, and performed a number of notable feats on the battlefield in 1643.

Their pike were especially formidable, and when deployed in massed bodies with their shot detached, as at Lansdowne, they attacked rapidly – which we represent by making the pike Determined Foot. Note that when combined with their shot their movement is restricted to that of the shot. Heavy casualties at the storming of Bristol, especially amongst their officers, reduced their ardour and they were never again the same force.

Royalist musketeer

EARLY ENGLISH CIVIL WAR ROYALIST STARTER ARMY		
Commander-in-Chief	1	Field Commander
Sub-Commanders	2	2 x Troop Commander
Horse	3 BG	4 bases of horse: Superior, Armoured, Cavaliers – Impact Pistol, Melee Pistol
Horse	1 BG	4 bases of horse: Average, Unarmoured, Cavaliers – Impact Pistol, Melee Pistol
Foot	4 BGs	Each comprising 6 bases of foot: 2 Average, Unarmoured, Heavy Foot – Pike; and 4 Average, Unarmoured, Medium Foot – Musket*
Commanded shot	2 BGs	Each comprising 2 bases of commanded shot: Average, Unarmoured, Medium Foot – Musket
Dragoons	1 BG	3 bases of dragoons: Average, Unarmoured, Dragoons – Musket
Camp	1	Unfortified camp
Total	11 BGs	Camp, 16 mounted bases, 31 foot bases, 3 commanders

BUILDING A CUSTOMISED LIST USING OUR ARMY POINTS

Choose an army based on the maxima and minima in the list below. The following special instructions apply to this army:

- Commanders should be depicted as Horse.
- Only one of the battle groups of horse in the Cornish army in 1643 can be Superior.
- Commanded out musketeers do not count as "commanded shot" as defined in the rules.

Prince Rupert's charge, 1642, by Graham Turner © Osprey Publishing Ltd. Taken from Campaign 82: Edgehill 1642.

EARLY ENGLISH CIVIL WAR ROYALIST

Territory Types: Agricultural, Hilly, Woodlands

C-in-C	Great Commander/Field Commander/Troop Commander					80/50/35	1	
Sub-commanders	Field Commander					50	0–2	
	Troop Commander					35	0–3	

Troop name		Troop Type			Capabilities			Points per base	Bases per BG	Total bases
		Type	Armour	Quality	Shooting	Impact	Melee			
Core Troops										
Horse	Only in 1642	Cavaliers	Armoured	Average	–	Pistol	Swordsmen	14	4	0–12	12–36
		Cavaliers	Unarmoured	Average	–	Pistol	Swordsmen	11	4	8–36
				Poor				8		
	Only from 1643	Cavaliers	Armoured	Superior	–	Pistol	Pistol	19	4	12–36
				Average				14		
				Poor				10		
		Cavaliers	Unarmoured	Superior	–	Pistol	Pistol	16	4	
				Average				11		
				Poor				8		
		Cavaliers	Unarmoured	Average	–	Pistol	Swordsmen	11	4	
				Poor				8		
Foot	Only in 1642	Medium Foot	Unarmoured	Average	Musket*	–	–	7	4	6	0–66	18–120
		Heavy Foot	Unarmoured	Average	–	Pike	Pike	5	2	
		Medium Foot	Unarmoured	Poor	Musket*	–	–	5	4	6	18–66
		Heavy Foot	Unarmoured	Poor	–	Pike	Pike	3	2	
	Only from 1643	Medium Foot	Unarmoured	Average	Musket*	–	–	7	4	6	12–72
		Heavy Foot	Unarmoured	Average	–	Pike	Pike	5	2	
		Medium Foot	Unarmoured	Poor	Musket*	–	–	5	4	6	
		Heavy Foot	Unarmoured	Poor	–	Pike	Pike	3	2	
Field artillery		Medium Artillery	–	Average	Medium Artillery	–	–	20	2	0–2	0–2
Light artillery		Light Artillery	–	Average	Light Artillery	–	–	12	2	0–2	
Optional Troops										
Commanded shot		Medium Foot	Unarmoured	Average	Musket	–	–	8	2	0–4
				Poor				6		
Dragoons	Any	Dragoons	Unarmoured	Average	Arquebus	–	–	7	3 or 4	0–6	0–6
	Only in 1642	Dragoons	Unarmoured	Average	Musket	–	–	8	3 or 4	0–3	
	Only from 1643									0–6	
Special Campaigns										
Only Cornish army in 1643										
Replace Foot with Cornish regiments		Medium Foot	Unarmoured	Superior	Musket*	–	–	10	4	6	All
		Determined Foot	Unarmoured	Superior	–	Pike	Pike	9	2	
Only rapid raiding force in 1643										
Only Horse, Dragoons (twice normal number may be used) and Commanded out musketeers (see below) allowed										
Commanded out musketeers		Medium Foot	Unarmoured	Average	Musket	–	–	7	6	0–18

ENGLISH CIVIL WAR PARLIAMENTARIAN

At the start of hostilities between King Charles and Parliament in 1642, the latter were much better placed to raise forces than was the King. There were a number of contributory factors to this. Firstly, Parliament held London which, in addition to being the capital, was the mercantile centre of the kingdom and had both the Tower of London armoury and an existing armaments industry. Secondly, the magazine city of Hull declared for Parliament, as did the navy, which was able to disrupt supplies arriving in England from the continent, where the Queen was raising money and supplies for the King. Lastly, following the outbreak of rebellion in Ireland in 1641, Parliament had been responsible for raising new troops to fight there, and so had been able to appoint, as far as possible, officers who would be favourable to them should a break with the King occur. All of this meant that by the autumn of 1642 Parliament had a significant force in the field well before the King.

Despite all these advantages, the war, when it came, did not start auspiciously for the Parliamentarians. The defeat of their cavalry at Powick Bridge gave them an inferiority complex that was not overcome for most of the war, with the exception of Oliver Cromwell's Ironsides of the Eastern Association.

The Westminster Trained Bands, 1643, by Angus McBride © Osprey Publishing Ltd. Taken from Elite 25: Soldiers of the English Civil War (1): Infantry.

Initially, like the King, Parliament organised its forces into a single field army with the expectation that the war would be concluded quickly. As it became clear that this would not be the case, groupings of counties were organised into "Associations", who were to raise, and maintain, additional armies to fight the Royalists in their locale. The main Associations were the Northern, Western and Eastern, with a Southern Association added later after the elimination of the western army. Undoubtedly the best of the Association armies was that of the Eastern Association, led by the Earl of Manchester, although it is most famous for its cavalry. The main Parliamentarian army, under the Earl of Essex, was not tied to an association. However, as it was mainly recruited from London and the south-east, plus was supported in the field by the London Trained Bands, it did not campaign far from the south of England with any regularity.

Following the drawn Battle of Edgehill, the only major engagement of 1642, Parliamentarian forces suffered a series of reverses in the north and south-west of England the following year. However, towards the end of 1643 things started to move more in the direction of Parliament. The campaign of the Earl of Essex, with the main Parliamentarian field army, that prevented the fall of Gloucester and fought its way past the King at the First Battle of Newbury, raised morale and showed that the Parliamentarian forces could face off the best the Royalists could throw at them. Even more encouragingly, the Eastern Association cavalry gained victories over the Royalist cavalry at Gainsborough and Winceby.

Haselrigge's Lobsters at Roundway Down, 1643, by Angus McBride © Osprey Publishing Ltd.
Taken from Elite 27: Soldiers of the English Civil War (2): Cavalry.

ENGLISH CIVIL WAR PARLIAMENTARIAN

The year of 1644 was the defining year of the war, although not in the way that it would first appear. With a truce negotiated by the King's representative in Ireland, a new source of trained troops was available to the Royalists, posing a threat to Parliament. However, a victory gained by Sir Thomas Fairfax at Nantwich in Cheshire destroyed the first of the Irish regiments shipped to England, starting the year well for the Parliamentarian armies. Additionally, in March Waller gained a victory at Cheriton over his old adversary, Hopton. With the threat of Irish manpower, not to mention Irish Catholicism, remaining, however, Parliament chose to enter into an alliance with the Scots Covenanters with the aim of adding their substantial army to Parliament's own, and thus bring the war to a successful conclusion. The cost of this alliance, in addition to cash, was to be the imposition of the Presbyterian Church on England. The Scots army crossed the border in January, and despite a set back when their cavalry was defeated at Corbridge, they joined with the armies of Fairfax and the Earl of Manchester to besiege the Royalist northern commander, the Marquis of Newcastle, in York. This resulted in the King sending Prince Rupert north to relieve York, which he did on 1st July. For reasons which are still controversial, Rupert then decided to fight the allied army, and caught them at Marston Moor the following day. There, thanks to the exploits of Cromwell's Eastern Association cavalry, he was decisively defeated, giving Parliament control of the north.

Despite these successes the war, rather unexpectedly, somewhat went against Parliament thereafter. At the end of June Waller lost the battle of Copredy Bridge, where he was outmanoeuvred by the King, and in the aftermath his army started to desert him. The troops that did remain suffered poor morale and often refused to march far from their homes. The Earl of Essex, with what was in theory the main Parliamentarian field army, decided to campaign in the west country, where his army was forced to surrender in humiliating circumstances at Lostwithiel in Cornwall, despite heavily outnumbering the Royalists. With the King suddenly in better circumstances than he had any right to be, Parliament combined the army of the Eastern Association, Waller and the remnants of Essex's army, and faced the King at the Second Battle of Newbury. Stiff resistance by the outnumbered Royalists, combined with dissention in the ranks of the Parliamentarian leadership, resulted in a stalemate which, given the situation, was tantamount to a victory for the King. The lasting result of this string of reverses was the realisation that a new army and structure was needed if the war was to be concluded. The result was the New Model Army.

This list covers English Civil War Parliamentarian armies other than the New Model army. Thus it covers the main armies, such as those of the Earl of Essex and Sir William Waller, and the small regional forces that remained after the formation of the New Model in 1645. The latter also covers the armies in Ireland, loyal to the English Parliament, that were significantly reinforced from 1647 onwards, until the victories of the Commonwealth field army in 1649/50 made their presence in the field unnecessary.

London Trained Band pikemen

TROOP NOTES

Following their early rout at Powick Bridge, the Parliamentarian cavalry, although well equipped, were easily outclassed by their Royalist counterparts, inspired by Prince Rupert. Through 1643, however, the situation improved, especially in the Eastern Association, where Cromwell's famous double strength "Ironsides" were raised. By the end of the year at Winceby they were able to defeat a strong Royalist cavalry force. By mid-1644, at the battle of Marston Moor, it is clear that the best of the Eastern Association horse were the equal to Prince Rupert's cavaliers. The tactics of the Eastern Association cavalry are described by John Vernon in "The Young Horseman" as:

"… all the Troops are to be drawn into battalia, each being not above three deepe, likewise each troop must be at least a hundred paces distance behind each other for the better avoiding of disorder, for those troops that are to give the first charge being drawn up in battail as before, are to be at their close order, every left hand mans right knee must be close locked under his right hand mans left ham, as has been shown before. In this order they are to advance towards the Enemy with an easie pace, firing their Carbines at a convenient distance, always aiming at their enemies breast or lower, because the powder is of an elevating nature, then drawing near the Enemy, they are with their right hands to take forth one of their pistols out of their houlsters, and holding the lock

London Trained Bands, 1643, by Graham Turner © Osprey Publishing Ltd. Taken from Campaign 116: First Newbury 1643.

uppermost firing as before, always reserving one Pistol ready, charged, spann'd and primed in your houlsters ... having thus fired the troops are to charge the Enemy in full career, but in good order with their swords fastned with a Riband or the like to their wrists ... still keeping in close order close locked ...".

The London Trained Bands regiments which took the field at Turnham Green, and also played an important role at First Newbury, were well equipped and of good morale, and are included in the Foot Regiments in this list. The London Auxiliary regiments were not always as effective, and can be represented by Poor quality foot battle groups.

At the start of the war, a number of cuirassier companies were formed, such as that of the Earl of Essex. The most famous of these was that of Sir Arthur Haselrigge, which became a whole regiment, his famous "Lobsters" – so called for their complete armour – the only such regiment of the whole war. They were destroyed at Roundway Down in 1643, and although Haselrigge raised a new regiment, this was conventionally armoured.

Parliamentarian foot regiments at the start of the war were usually well equipped and many had sufficient numbers of pikemen's corselets to justify Armoured classification. However, as with most armies of the period, these were soon discarded as cumbersome, heavy and uncomfortable.

The foot regiments of the Northern Association army that fought at Adwalton Moor in 1643 were comprised of nearly all musketeers rather than the usual pike and shot arrangements.

ENGLISH CIVIL WAR PARLIAMENTARIAN (LATE 1643) STARTER ARMY

Commander-in-Chief	1	Field Commander
Sub-Commanders	2	2 x Troop Commander
Haselrigge's "Lobsters"	1 BG	4 bases of "Lobsters": Average, Heavily Armoured, Horse – Impact Pistol, Melee Pistol
Horse	2 BGs	Each comprising 4 bases of horse: Average, Armoured, Horse – Impact Pistol, Melee Pistol
Horse	1 BG	4 bases of horse: Average, Armoured, Horse – Carbine, Melee Pistol
Foot	5 BGs	Each comprising 6 bases of foot: 2 Average, Unarmoured, Heavy Foot – Pike; and 4 Average, Unarmoured, Medium Foot – Musket
Commanded shot	2 BGs	Each comprising 2 bases of commanded shot: Average, Unarmoured, Medium Foot – Musket
Dragoons	1 BG	3 bases of dragoons: Average, Unarmoured, Dragoons – Musket
Field artillery	1 BG	2 bases of field artillery: Average, Medium Artillery – Medium Artillery
Camp	1	Unfortified camp
Total	13 BGs	Camp, 16 mounted bases, 39 foot bases, 3 commanders

BUILDING A CUSTOMISED LIST USING OUR ARMY POINTS

Choose an army based on the maxima and minima in the list below. The following special instructions apply to this army:

* Commanders should be depicted as Horse.

* A Northern Association army in 1643 cannot include any Eastern Association troops.
* All cuirassiers must have the same capabilities.
* Cuirassiers cannot be used with Ironsides.

ENGLISH CIVIL WAR PARLIAMENTARIAN

Territory Types: Agricultural, Hilly, Woodlands

C-in-C	Great Commander/Field Commander/Troop Commander		80/50/35	1
Sub-commanders	Field Commander		50	0–2
	Troop Commander		35	0–3

Troop name		Troop Type			Capabilities			Points per base	Bases per BG	Total bases
		Type	Armour	Quality	Shooting	Impact	Melee			
Core Troops										
Horse	Only in 1642	Horse	Armoured	Poor	Carbine	–	Pistol	8	4	8–40
	Only from 1643	Horse	Armoured	Average	Carbine	–	Pistol	11	4	0–40
			Armoured	Poor				8		
			Unarmoured	Poor				7		
	Only from late 1643	Horse	Armoured	Average	–	Pistol	Pistol	10	4	8–40
	Only Eastern Association horse (Ironsides) in late 1643	Determined Horse	Armoured	Superior	–	Pistol	Pistol	21	4	0–8
	Only Eastern Association horse in 1644	Determined Horse	Armoured	Superior	–	Pistol	Pistol	21	4	0–20
				Average				15		
Foot	Only in 1642	Medium Foot	Unarmoured	Average	Musket	–	–	8	4	6	0–60	18–96
		Heavy Foot	Armoured	Average	–	Pike	Pike	6	2		
		Medium Foot	Unarmoured	Poor	Musket	–	–	6	4	6	18–36
		Heavy Foot	Armoured	Poor	–	Pike	Pike	4	2		
		Medium Foot	Unarmoured	Poor	Musket*	–	–	5	4	6	0–36
		Heavy Foot	Unarmoured	Poor	–	Pike	Pike	3	2		
Foot	Only from 1643	Medium Foot	Unarmoured	Average	Musket	–	–	8	4	6	12–96	12–96
		Heavy Foot	Unarmoured	Average	–	Pike	Pike	5	2		
		Medium Foot	Unarmoured	Poor	Musket	–	–	6	4	6	12–96
		Heavy Foot	Unarmoured	Poor	–	Pike	Pike	3	2		
Veteran Foot	Only in 1644	Medium Foot	Unarmoured	Superior	Musket	–	–	11	4	6	0–12
		Heavy Foot	Unarmoured	Superior	–	Pike	Pike	8	2		
Field artillery		Medium Artillery	–	Average	Medium Artillery	–	–	20	2	0–2	2–4
Light artillery		Light Artillery	–	Average	Light Artillery	–	–	12	2	0–2	
Optional Troops										
Cuirassiers	Only before 1644	Horse	Heavily Armoured	Average	–	Pistol	Pistol	12	2 or 4	0–4
					Carbine	–	Pistol	13		
Commanded shot		Medium Foot	Unarmoured	Average	Musket	–	–	8	2	0–4
				Poor				6		
Dragoons		Dragoons	Unarmoured	Average	Musket	–	–	8	3 or 4	0–6
				Poor				6		
Special Campaigns										
Only Northern Association in 1643										
Replace Foot with musketeer regiments		Medium Foot	Unarmoured	Average	Musket	–	–	7	6	¾ – all of foot BGs
Poorly armed levies		Mob	Unarmoured	Poor	–	–	–	2	6–8	0–8

LATER ENGLISH CIVIL WAR ROYALIST

This list covers English Civil War Royalist armies from when the beneficial effects of the capture of Bristol in July 1643 were felt by some of the Royalist forces, notably the Oxford army and forces in the English midlands. The major difference from early war armies was that there were now sufficient firearms to properly equip the armies and, indeed, some Royalist infantry units appear to have been wholly musket armed by the end of the war. Despite the better availability of firearms, some regional forces remained less well equipped, and these are covered by the Early English Civil War list.

Despite the capture of Bristol and the benefits this brought, this realistically marked the high point of Royalist fortunes in the war. This was demonstrated shortly afterwards when they failed to take Gloucester, probably due to a reluctance to storm a defended city after the severe losses at Bristol, and then also failed to defeat the Earl of Essex at the First Battle of Newbury, despite having a superior strategic position, by being between the Earl and his London base. The reality was that Parliament still controlled the more prosperous and populated areas of the country, and thus had an economic advantage.

However, under orders from the King, the Duke of Ormonde, Lord Lieutenant of Ireland, negotiated a cessation of hostilities with the Irish, which freed up experienced soldiers who could be shipped to England to fight for the King. This was, however, easier said than done. With Parliament controlling the navy, shipping troops in any numbers was difficult, and when they did land Irish soldiers were even less popular with civilians than English ones. Although a few thousand troops were brought to England, many

were lost at Nantwich in January 1644, and the rest were too few to change the course of the war.

1644 also saw the largest battle of the war, at Marston Moor in Yorkshire. After breaking the siege of York, Prince Rupert decided to fight the larger allied army of Scots and Parliamentarians and was soundly beaten. It is not entirely clear why Rupert felt he had to fight this battle, as the alliance of the Scots and Parliamentarians was anything but cordial, and their army was on the verge of separating into its constituent parts, which might have been neutralised individually. Rupert always claimed his orders from the King stated that he should fight, and for some time afterwards he carried these with him to justify his decision. The result was, however, that the north was lost to the King and, in effect, occupied by the Scots for the remainder of the war.

Lord George Goring

Royalist cavalry, 1645, by Angus McBride © Osprey Publishing Ltd. Taken from Elite 27: Soldiers of the English Civil War (2): Cavalry.

In the south the King was faced by two major Parliamentarian armies under the Earl of Essex and Sir William Waller. These failed to act in close co-operation, however, and, remarkably, the King was able to defeat both of them, firstly Waller at Cropredy Bridge, and then Essex in Cornwall at Lostwithiel, where the entirety of Essex's foot were forced to surrender and lay down their arms. The subsequent Second Battle of Newbury again showed the fighting spirit of the Royalist army, as it beat off the combined forces of the Eastern Association and Parliament's sundry troops from the south of England.

Despite 1644 ending remarkably well for the King, his strategic position was still weak. To add to his difficulties, Parliament had moved to put its army on a sounder footing with the creation of the New Model Army. The two armies met at Naseby in June of that year. Despite the improvements in the quality of the Parliamentarian cavalry, Prince Rupert's troopers were again victorious, but as usual chased their defeated enemy from the field and headed towards the baggage train rather than turning on the flank of the infantry. The rest of the Royalist cavalry, facing Cromwell on the opposite wing, also fought well, but superior numbers prevailed and they were defeated. In the infantry fight the Royalists were initially successful, penetrating the first line of the New Model foot, however, they were also stalled by superior numbers and fell back. The superior control Cromwell had over his cavalry now proved decisive as, unlike Rupert's troopers, Cromwell's did turn into the flank of the Royalist foot. Despite a desperate last stand by the King's Lifeguard and Rupert's "Blewcoats", both foot regiments, the result was

inevitable and the last effective Royalist field army was destroyed.

Despite further actions around the country, Naseby to all intents ended the war, and in 1646 Charles surrendered himself to the Scots army at Newark, rather than to the English Parliamentarians.

TROOP NOTES

With an increased supply of muskets and a need for rapid movement, the Royalist armies, no doubt under Prince Rupert's influence, started to make use of large bodies of "commanded out" shot – that is musketeers operating independently from their regiment's pike. An example of the scale of this is the start of the campaign that led to the Battle of Cropredy Bridge, when the army that marched from Oxford comprised of 5,000 horse and 2,500 musketeers. The remaining infantry (1,500 musketeers and 200 pike) joined the army on the march somewhat later. In addition to this, a number of foot regiments appear to have been made up of just musketeers, possibly because they had been created out of garrison forces who had little need of pikes.

Firelocks are traditionally assumed to have been used to guard the artillery train, as they are safer around gunpowder, lacking the burning match of the matchlock musket. In the Royalist army, however, they became a form of assault troops, some gaining a fearsome reputation. This may have been due to the fact that they often contained a significant Irish contingent, who were motivated by the fact that if captured by the Parliamentarians they would be hanged forthwith. Another use for firelock companies was as bodyguards for senior officers – both Prince Rupert and Prince Maurice had such guards.

LATER ENGLISH CIVIL WAR ROYALIST (1644) STARTER ARMY		
Commander-in-Chief	1	Field Commander
Sub-Commanders	2	2 x Troop Commander
Horse	2 BGs	Each comprising 4 bases of horse: Superior, Armoured, Cavaliers – Impact Pistol, Melee Pistol
Horse	2 BGs	Each comprising 4 bases of horse: Average, Unarmoured, Cavaliers – Impact Pistol, Melee Pistol
Foot	1 BG	6 bases of foot: 2 Superior, Unarmoured, Heavy Foot – Pike; and 4 Superior, Unarmoured, Medium Foot – Musket
Foot	2 BGs	Each comprising 6 bases of foot: 2 Average, Unarmoured, Heavy Foot – Pike; and 4 Average, Unarmoured, Medium Foot – Musket
Firelocks	1 BG	4 bases of firelocks: Superior, Unarmoured, Medium Foot – Musket
Commanded shot	2 BGs	Each comprising 2 bases of commanded shot: Average, Unarmoured Medium Foot – Musket
Dragoons	1 BG	3 bases of dragoons: Average, Unarmoured, Dragoons – Musket
Camp	1	Unfortified camp
Total	11 BGs	Camp, 16 mounted bases, 29 foot bases, 3 commanders

Royalist and Parliamentary cavalry, 1643, by Graham Turner © Osprey Publishing Ltd. Taken from Campaign 116: First Newbury 1643.

BUILDING A CUSTOMISED LIST USING OUR ARMY POINTS

Choose an army based on the maxima and minima in the list below. The following special instructions apply to this army:

- Commanders should be depicted as Horse.

- Commanded out musketeers do not count as "commanded shot" as defined in the rules.
- An army containing no Pike bases must have more mounted and Dragoon bases than infantry and artillery bases. Commanders' bases do not count as any of these.

LATER ENGLISH CIVIL WAR ROYALIST									
Territory Types: Agricultural, Hilly, Woodlands									
C-in-C	Great Commander/Field Commander/Troop Commander						80/50/35	1	
Sub-commanders	Field Commander						50	0–2	
	Troop Commander						35	0–3	
Troop name	Troop Type			Capabilities			Points per base	Bases per BG	Total bases
	Type	Armour	Quality	Shooting	Impact	Melee			
Core Troops									
Horse	Cavaliers	Armoured	Superior	–	Pistol	Pistol	19	4	16–42
			Average				14		
			Poor				10		
	Cavaliers	Unarmoured	Superior	–	Pistol	Pistol	16	4	
			Average				11		
			Poor				8		
	Cavaliers	Unarmoured	Average	–	Pistol	Swordsmen	11	4	
			Poor				8		
Foot regiments or commanded out musketeers	Medium Foot	Unarmoured	Average	Musket	–	–	8	4	6	12–36
	Heavy Foot	Unarmoured	Average	–	Pike	Pike	5	2	
	Medium Foot	Unarmoured	Poor	Musket	–	–	6	4	6
	Heavy Foot	Unarmoured	Poor	–	Pike	Pike	3	2	
	Medium Foot	Unarmoured	Average	Musket	–	–	7	6	
			Poor				5		
Veteran foot regiments or commanded out musketeers	Only from 1644	Medium Foot	Unarmoured	Superior	Musket	–	–	11	4	6	0–18	12–72
		Heavy Foot	Unarmoured	Superior	–	Pike	Pike	8	2	
		Medium Foot	Unarmoured	Superior	Musket	–	–	10	6	
Regional foot regiments	Medium Foot	Unarmoured	Average	Musket*	–	–	7	4	6	0–48
	Heavy Foot	Unarmoured	Average	–	Pike	Pike	5	2	
	Medium Foot	Unarmoured	Poor	Musket*	–	–	5	4	6
	Heavy Foot	Unarmoured	Poor	–	Pike	Pike	3	2	
Field artillery	Medium Artillery	–	Average	Medium Artillery	–	–	20	2	0–2	0–2
Light artillery	Light Artillery	–	Average	Light Artillery	–	–	12	2	0–2	
Optional Troops									
Commanded shot	Medium Foot	Unarmoured	Average	Musket	–	–	8	2	0–4
			Poor				6		
Dragoons	Dragoons	Unarmoured	Average	Musket	–	–	8	3 or 4	0–6
Firelocks	Medium Foot	Unarmoured	Superior	Musket	–	–	10	4	0–4

NEW MODEL ARMY

*B*y the end of 1644, prompted by the failure of their combined armies to defeat the King at the Second Battle of Newbury, Parliament decided that a radical overhaul of their forces was needed to force a decision in what was becoming a drawn out war. The result of this was a "new modelling" of the main field army of Parliament, drawing on the best of the soldiers from the armies of Essex, Waller and the Eastern Association to form a hopefully war-winning force. This was accompanied by the Self Denying Ordinance, whereby members of Parliament, of both the House of Commons and the House of Lords, debarred themselves from military command in order to remove politics from military command – although Oliver Cromwell was given a dispensation from this as Sir Thomas Fairfax requested he be allowed to fill the role of Lieutenant-General of the Cavalry. Thus the "New Model Army" was created. The planned strength of the army was to be 11 regiments of horse, each of 600 troopers, 12 regiments of foot, each of 1,200 men, and a single regiment of dragoons of 1,000 men. Additionally, an artillery train would be provided. Those soldiers not incorporated into the new army would remain in subsidiary regional forces.

Despite being able to draw on three existing armies for its recruits, the army was still rather under strength when it took the field in 1645.

The New Model Army, 1645, by Angus McBride © Osprey Publishing Ltd. Taken from Elite 25: Soldiers of the English Civil War (1): Infantry.

Cavalry numbers were easily reached, but the infantry numbers were very low. Despite a ruthless impressment campaign, they were still below establishment at the Battle of Naseby – at which, nevertheless, the New Model Army was victorious, finally destroying any chance the King had of winning the war.

Following the end of the First Civil War, Parliament chose to retain a standing army, the first significant standing force ever maintained by England. Following the end of the war, however, the army became radicalised by Protestant non-conformists and started to intervene in politics. This significantly affected the English view of standing armies, and her politicians remained suspicious of such standing forces thereafter.

Subsequently the army fought in Ireland (1649–1652), in Scotland (1650), England (against invading Scots in 1651 and various Royalist uprisings) and, strangely, in support of Catholic France (1654) against Spain. English infantry and naval gunfire were important in Turenne's victory at the Battle of the Dunes. An army was also sent to the West Indies in 1654 as part of the war against Spain.

Ironically, after playing such a major part in the defeat and overthrow of Charles I, the army was then instrumental, under General George Monck,

in restoring his son to the throne as Charles II. Following the restoration, most of the army was disbanded.

The first Lord-General of the New Model was Sir Thomas Fairfax, with Oliver Cromwell as Lieutenant-General of the Cavalry and Philip Skippon as Sergeant-Major General of the Foot. Cromwell later took over as Lord-General in 1649 when Sir Thomas declined the command of the army to campaign in Ireland.

This list covers the English army of Parliament from the creation of the "New Model Army" in 1645, through the army of the English Commonwealth, until most of the standing army was demobilised following the restoration of King Charles II in 1660. The army sent to the West Indies in 1654 is covered by a later list in Field of Glory Renaissance Companion 6: *Cities of Gold*.

TROOP NOTES

Despite being partly drawn from existing armies, the quality of the New Model infantry was not high. This appears to be because many of the soldiers were in fact impressed Royalists and rounded-up deserters. The cavalry, on the other hand, was a quality force based around the formidable Eastern Association troops.

NEW MODEL ARMY STARTER ARMY			
Commander-in-Chief	1	Field Commander	
Sub-Commanders	2	2 x Troop Commander	
Horse	2 BGs	Each comprising 4 bases of horse: Superior, Armoured, Determined Horse – Impact Pistol, Melee Pistol	
Horse	2 BGs	Each comprising 4 bases of horse: Average, Armoured, Determined Horse – Impact Pistol, Melee Pistol	
Foot	3 BGs	Each comprising 6 bases of foot: 2 Average, Unarmoured, Heavy Foot – Pike; and 4 Average, Unarmoured, Medium Foot – Musket	
Dragoons	1 BG	3 bases of dragoons: Average, Unarmoured, Dragoons – Musket	
Field artillery	1 BG	2 bases of field artillery: Average, Medium Artillery – Medium Artillery	
Camp	1	Unfortified camp	
Total	9 BGs	Camp, 16 mounted bases, 23 foot bases, 3 commanders	

BUILDING A CUSTOMISED LIST USING OUR ARMY POINTS

Choose an army based on the maxima and minima in the list below. The following special instructions apply to this army:

• Commanders should be depicted as Horse.

NEW MODEL ARMY									
Territory Types: Agricultural, Hilly, Woodlands									
C-in-C	Great Commander/Field Commander/Troop Commander						80/50/35	1	
Sub-commanders	Field Commander						50	0–2	
	Troop Commander						35	0–3	
Troop name	Troop Type			Capabilities			Points per base	Bases per BG	Total bases
	Type	Armour	Quality	Shooting	Impact	Melee			
Core Troops									
Horse	Determined horse	Armoured	Superior	–	Pistol	Pistol	21	4	8–32
			Average				15		
Foot	Medium Foot	Unarmoured	Average	Musket	–	–	8	4	12–64
	Heavy Foot	Unarmoured	Average	–	Pike	Pike	5	2	6
Veteran Foot	Only from 1646	Medium Foot	Unarmoured	Superior	Musket	–	–	11	4	0–18
		Heavy Foot	Unarmoured	Superior	–	Pike	Pike	8	2	6
Field artillery	Medium Artillery	–	Average	Medium Artillery	–	–	20	2	0–2
Light artillery	Light Artillery	–	Average	Light Artillery	–	–	12	2	0–2
Optional Troops									
Dragoons	Dragoons	Unarmoured	Average	Musket	–	–	8	3 or 4	0–6
Firelocks	Medium Foot	Unarmoured	Average	Musket	–	–	7	4	0–4
Association or militia horse	Determined horse	Armoured	Average	–	Pistol	Pistol	15	4	0–8
			Poor				11		
Association or militia foot	Medium Foot	Unarmoured	Poor	Musket	–	–	6	4	0–18
	Heavy Foot	Unarmoured	Poor	–	Pike	Pike	3	2	6

Note: Foot total bases 12–72; Veteran Foot 0–72; artillery combined 0–4.

NEW MODEL ARMY ALLIES									
Allied commander	Field Commander/Troop Commander						40/25	1	
Troop name	Troop Type			Capabilities			Points per base	Bases per BG	Total bases
	Type	Armour	Quality	Shooting	Impact	Melee			
Horse	Determined Horse	Armoured	Superior	–	Pistol	Pistol	21	4	4–12
			Average				15		
Foot	Medium Foot	Unarmoured	Average	Musket	–	–	8	4	6–24
	Heavy Foot	Unarmoured	Average	–	Pike	Pike	5	2	6
Veteran Foot	Only from 1646	Medium Foot	Unarmoured	Superior	Musket	–	–	11	4	0–6
		Heavy Foot	Unarmoured	Superior	–	Pike	Pike	8	2	6

NEW MODEL ARMY

Cavalry of the New Model Army, 1645, by Angus McBride © Osprey Publishing Ltd. Taken from Elite 27:
Soldiers of the English Civil War (2): Cavalry.

EARLY LOUIS XIV FRENCH

This list covers French armies from the outbreak of the Frondes series of civil wars (1648–1653) until Louis XIV took over personal control of the government after the death of Cardinal Mazarin in 1661, which allowed Louis to dictate military matters.

During most of this period the French were at war with the Spanish in the Low Countries and, to a much lesser extent, in Catalonia. In addition, from 1648 to 1653 there were a series of civil wars in France, which are known as the Frondes – from *fronde*, meaning a sling, which was used by rioters in Paris at the start of the first civil war.

The Frondes were notable in that the two best French generals, Turenne and Condé, were both in opposition to the government of Cardinal Mazarin and the Queen Mother, Anne of Austria. However, in 1650 Turenne, realising he was being manipulated, asked for a pardon from the young Louis XIV, which he received. He then led the Royal armies to defeat the rebels, whilst Condé actually entered Spanish service.

The war with Spain was finally decided following the Spanish defeat at the Battle of the Dunes in 1658. The battle saw a French army led by Turenne, with allies supplied by the Protestant Commonwealth of England, face a Spanish army which included French cavalry and infantry led by Condé. The subsequent Treaty of the Pyrenees which brought the war to a mostly satisfactory conclusion for France, also saw Condé pardoned by Louis and re-enter French service.

TROOP NOTES

During this period, under the guidance of Turenne and Condé, French cavalry appear to have started to use a more aggressive "sword in hand" approach to combat, although this may not have applied to all. At the same time, however, they gained a reputation for being somewhat ill-disciplined and this was only stamped out later in Louis XIV's reign when Turenne was Colonel-Général of Cavalry. Because of this ill-discipline we classify them as Cavaliers.

EARLY LOUIS XIV FRENCH STARTER ARMY		
Commander-in-Chief	1	Field Commander
Sub-Commanders	2	2 x Troop Commander
Chevaux-légers, gendarmerie or similar	1 BG	4 bases of chevaux-légers, gendarmerie or carabins: Superior, Armoured, Determined Horse – Impact Pistol, Melee Pistol
Chevaux-légers, gendarmerie or similar	2 BGs	Each comprising 4 bases of chevaux-légers, gendarmerie or carabins: Superior, Unarmoured, Cavaliers – Impact Mounted, Melee Pistol
Dragoons	1 BG	3 bases of dragoons: Average, Unarmoured Dragoons – Musket
Guard and Vieux infantry	1 BG	6 bases of guard and vieux infantry: 2 Superior, Unarmoured, Heavy Foot – Pike; and 4 Superior, Unarmoured, Medium Foot – Musket*, Impact Foot
Petits Vieux and other infantry	2 BGs	Each comprising 6 bases of petits vieux and other infantry: 2 Average, Unarmoured, Heavy Foot – Pike; and 4 Average, Unarmoured, Medium Foot – Musket*, Impact Foot
Petits Vieux and other infantry	1 BG	6 bases of petits vieux and other infantry: Average, Unarmoured, Medium Foot – Musket*, Impact Foot
Artillery	1 BG	2 bases of artillery: Average Medium Artillery – Medium Artillery
Camp	1	Unfortified camp
Total	9 BGs	Camp, 12 mounted bases, 29 foot bases, 3 commanders

BUILDING A CUSTOMISED LIST USING OUR ARMY POINTS

Choose an army based on the maxima and minima in the list below. The following special instructions apply to this army:

- Commanders should be depicted as Chevaux-légers.

- The minimum marked * is reduced to 4 for rebel armies before 1653.
- Only Royal armies can use Armoured infantry.
- If English warships are used the English allies must also be used.
- Cavaliers, Superior infantry and Superior Determined Horse cannot be used with the Catalan War special campaign options.

EARLY LOUIS XIV FRENCH									
Territory Types: Agricultural, Woodland, Hilly									
C-in-C	Great Commander/Field Commander/Troop Commander						80/50/35		1
Sub-commanders	Field Commander						50		0–2
	Troop Commander						35		0–3
Troop name	Troop Type			Capabilities			Points per base	Bases per BG	Total bases
	Type	Armour	Quality	Shooting	Impact	Melee			
Core Troops									
Chevaux-légers, gendarmerie or similar	Cavaliers	Armoured	Superior	–	Impact Mounted	Swordsmen	21	4	*8–36
	Cavaliers	Unarmoured	Superior	–	Impact Mounted	Swordsmen	18	4	
	Determined Horse	Armoured	Superior	–	Pistol	Pistol	21	4	
			Average				15		
	Determined Horse	Unarmoured	Superior	–	Pistol	Pistol	18	4	
			Average				12		
German cavalry	Only rebel armies before 1653	Determined Horse	Armoured	Average	–	Pistol	Pistol	15	4	4–12
		Determined Horse	Unarmoured	Average	–	Pistol	Pistol	12	4	
Dragoons	Dragoons	Unarmoured	Average	Musket	–	–	8	3 or 4	0–8
Guard and Vieux infantry	Medium Foot	Unarmoured	Superior	Musket*	Impact Foot		11	4	6	0–18
	Heavy Foot	Armoured	Superior	–	Pike	Pike	9	2	
	Medium Foot	Unarmoured	Superior	Musket*	Impact Foot		11	4	6
	Heavy Foot	Unarmoured	Superior	–	Pike	Pike	8	2	
Petits Vieux and other infantry	Medium Foot	Unarmoured	Average	Musket*	Impact Foot		8	4	6	12–36	12–60
	Heavy Foot	Unarmoured	Average	–	Pike	Pike	5	2	
	Medium Foot	Unarmoured	Average	Musket*	Impact Foot	–	7	6	0–36
Artillery	Heavy Artillery	–	Average	Heavy Artillery	–	–	25	2,3 or 4	2–4
	Medium Artillery	–	Average	Medium Artillery	–	–	20	2,3 or 4	
	Light Artillery	–	Average	Light Artillery	–	–	12	2,3 or 4	

Optional Troops										
Newly raised French infantry and militia	Medium Foot	Unarmoured	Poor	Musket*	Impact Foot	–	6	4	6	0–36
	Heavy Foot	Unarmoured	Poor	–	Pike	Pike	3	2		
Foreign infantry regiments	Medium Foot	Unarmoured	Average	Musket	–	–	8	4	6	0–24
	Heavy foot	Unarmoured	Average	–	Pike	Pike	5	2		
Special Campaigns										
Only Royal Army in 1658										
English warships	Naval Units	–	Average	Naval	–	–	30	–		0–1
English allies (no mounted BGs) – New Model Army										
Catalan War before 1658 (Royal army)										
Catalan militia	Only before 1653	Medium Foot	Unarmoured	Average	Musket	–	–	8	4	6	0–18
		Heavy Foot	Unarmoured	Average	–	Pike	Pike	5	2		
		Medium Foot	Unarmoured	Poor	Musket	–	–	6	4	6	
		Heavy Foot	Unarmoured	Poor	–	Pike	Pike	3	2		
Miquelets	Light Foot	Unarmoured	Average	Musket	–	–	7	6		6–18

EARLY LOUIS XIV FRENCH ALLIES

Allied commander		Field Commander/Troop Commander					40/25	1	
Troop name		**Troop Type**			**Capabilities**			**Points per base**	**Bases per BG**	**Total bases**
	Type	**Armour**	**Quality**	**Shooting**	**Impact**	**Melee**			
Chevaux-légers, gendarmerie or similar	Cavaliers	Armoured	Superior	–	Impact Mounted	Pistol	21	4	4–16
	Cavaliers	Unarmoured	Superior	–	Impact Mounted	Pistol	18	4	
	Determined Horse	Armoured	Superior	–	Pistol	Pistol	21	4	
			Average				15		
	Determined Horse	Unarmoured	Superior	–	Pistol	Pistol	18	4	
			Average				12		
German cavalry	Only rebel armies before 1653	Determined Horse	Armoured	Average	–	Pistol	Pistol	15	4	0–4
		Determined Horse	Unarmoured	Average	–	Pistol	Pistol	12	4	
Dragoons	Dragoons	Unarmoured	Average	Musket	–	–	8	3 or 4	0–4
Petits Vieux and other infantry	Medium Foot	Unarmoured	Average	Musket*	Impact Foot	–	8	4	6	6–18	6–30
	Heavy Foot	Unarmoured	Average	–	Pike	Pike	5	2		
	Medium Foot	Unarmoured	Average	Musket*	Impact Foot	–	7	6	0–18
Artillery	Medium Artillery	–	Average	Medium Artillery	–	–	20	2	0–2

APPENDIX 1 – USING THE LISTS

To give balanced games, armies can be selected using the points system. The more effective the troops, the more each base costs in points. The maximum points for an army will usually be set at between 600 and 800 points for a singles game for 2 to 4 hours play. We recommend 800 points for 15mm singles tournament games (650 points for 25mm) and between 900 and 1000 points for 15mm doubles games.

The army lists specify which troops can be used in a particular army. No other troops can be used. The number of bases of each type in the army must conform to the specified minima and maxima. Troops that have restrictions on when they can be used cannot be used with troops with a conflicting restriction. For example, troops that can only be used "before 1640" cannot be used with troops that can only be used "from 1640". All special instructions

applying to an army list must be adhered to. They also apply to allied contingents supplied by the army.

All armies must have a C-in-C and at least one other commander. No army can have more than 4 commanders in total, including C-in-C, sub-commanders and allied commanders.

All armies must have a supply camp. This is free unless fortified. A fortified camp can only be used if specified in the army list. Field fortifications and portable defences can only be used if specified in the army list.

Allied contingents can only be used if specified in the army list. Most allied contingents have their own allied contingent list, to which they must conform unless the main army's list specifies otherwise.

French infantry

BATTLE GROUPS

All troops are organized into battle groups. Commanders, supply camps and field fortifications are not troops and are not assigned to battle groups. Portable defences are not troops, but are assigned to specific battle groups.

Battle groups must comply with the following restrictions:

- The number of bases in a battle group must correspond to the range specified in the list.
- Each battle group must initially comprise an even number of bases (not counting regimental gun markers), with the following exceptions. These can only be used if specified by the list:
  - A battle group can only initially have 3 bases if this is explicitly stated in the list. e.g. If the battle group size is specified in the form "2,3,4", and not if specified in the form "2-4".
  - A battle group can only initially have 7 bases if it is specified in the list as a Swedish brigade formation.

- A battle group can only initially have 9 bases if this is explicitly stated in the list. e.g. If the battle group size is specified in the form "6,9,12", and not if specified in the form "6-12".
- A battle group can only include troops from one line in a list, unless the list specifies a mixed formation by indicating the battle group to be of types from more than one line. e.g. 6 musketeers & 3 pike or 4 musketeers & 2 pike – as in the list example below.
- All troops in a battle group must be of the same quality. Where a choice of quality is given in a list, this allows battle groups to differ from each other. It does not override the above rule for each battle group.
- All troops in a battle group with the same troop type and combat capabilities must be of the same armour class. Where a choice of armour class is given in a list, this allows battle groups to differ from each other. It does not override the above rule for each battle group.

Troop name		Troop Type			Capabilities			Points per base	Bases per BG	Total bases
		Type	Armour	Quality	Shooting	Impact	Melee			
Cuirassiers	Any date	Horse	Heavily Armoured	Superior	–	Pistol	Pistol	16	4	4–12
	Only from 1629	Horse	Armoured	Superior	–	Pistol	Pistol	13	4	
Arquebusiers		Horse	Armoured	Average	Carbine	–	Pistol	11	4–6	4–12
			Unarmoured					9		
Infantry regiments	Only before 1629	Medium Foot	Unarmoured	Average	Musket	–	–	8	6	9 (LT)	9–60
		Heavy Foot	Armoured	Average	–	Pike	Pike	6	3	
	Only from 1625	Medium Foot	Unarmoured	Average	Musket	–	–	8	4	6
		Heavy Foot	Armoured	Average	–	Pike	Pike	6	2	
Field guns		Medium Artillery	–	Average	Medium Artillery	–	–	20	2, 3 or 4	2–4

EXAMPLE LIST

Here is a section of an actual army list, which will help us to explain the basics and some special features. The list specifies the following items for each historical type included in the army:

- Troop Type – comprising Type, Armour and Quality.
- Capabilities – comprising Shooting, Impact and Melee capabilities.
- Points cost per base.
- Minimum and maximum number of bases in each battle group.
- Minimum and maximum number of bases in the army.

SPECIAL FEATURES:

- From 1629, Cuirassiers can be fielded as either Heavily Armoured or Armoured, but before that date can only be Heavily Armoured. Different battle groups can have different Armour rating (from 1629), but all the bases in each battle group must have the same Armour rating.
- Cuirassiers must always be fielded in battle groups of 4 bases. The army must include a minimum of 4 bases of Cuirassiers and may include up to 12.
- Arquebusiers can be fielded as either Armoured or Unarmoured, but all the bases in a battle group must be rated in the same way i.e. all Armoured or all Unarmoured. Different battle groups can have different Armour rating.
- Arquebusiers must be organized in battle groups of 4 or 6 bases, but the battle groups

do not all have to be the same size, i.e. a battle group of 4 bases and a battle group of 6 bases can be used in the same army. They cannot be fielded as 5 base battle groups.

- Before 1625, all Infantry regiments must be fielded as 9 base battle groups comprising 3 bases of pike and 6 bases of musketeers. These fight in the Later Tercio formation, as is indicated by the "(LT)" in the Bases per BG column.
- From 1629, Infantry regiments cannot be 9 bases strong and can only be fielded as 6 base battle groups comprising 2 bases of pike and 4 bases of musketeers. 6 base Infantry regiment battle groups are not Tercios.
- From 1625 to 1628 inclusive, Infantry regiments can be fielded as either 9 base battle groups or 6 base battle groups as the player wishes. Different sized battle groups can be fielded at the same time.
- The army must contain at least 9 Infantry regiment bases and cannot have more than 60. This minimum and maximum apply to the total number of Infantry regiment bases fielded regardless of which size or combination of size battle groups are fielded.
- Field guns can be organised in battle groups of 2, 3 or 4 bases. A 3 base battle group is allowed in this case because it is explicitly stated in the army list. If the list had "2-4" in the Bases per BG column, a battle group of 3 would not be allowed. The army must have between 2 and 4 bases of Field guns.

INDEX

INDEX

INDEX